From bestselling cookbook author Julia Turshen comes an original, inspired, and instructional approach to cooking that takes the guesswork out of everyday meals.

Known for her simple, practical, yet utterly satisfying recipes, Julia Turshen is a home cook's best friend. Whether you're looking for easy weeknight dinner ideas or for fail-safe dishes to shake up your repertoire, hers are the recipes that save the day. That's because Julia has an intuitive understanding of *what goes with what*—and now she wants to share that skill with you.

In *What Goes with What*, Julia offers the secrets to understanding how to pair, layer, and combine ingredients in ways that transform the contents of your fridge into an exciting meal. Using a series of charts to explain the alchemy of a dish, Julia explores everything from the anatomy of a satisfying salad (base + crunchy thing + rich thing + dressing) to meatballs (meat + binding + seasoning + sauce/glaze) to fruit cobblers (fruit + seasoning/thickener + fat/liquid + dry topping).

The result isn't just a collection of recipes but a whole new way to think about and understand cooking. From salads and sandwiches to soups, stews, and braises, from rice, grains, and pasta to vegetables, mains, and baked goods, Julia shares twenty charts and one hundred recipes that will both teach you how to cook a successful dish and offer endless possibilities for iteration and interpretation.

For readers of Samin Nosrat's classic *Salt, Fat, Acid, Heat* as well as foundational cookbooks like Sohla El-Waylly's *Start Here* and Claire Saffitz's *Dessert Person*, *What Goes with What* is an essential, must-have cookbook in any home cook's collection.

ALSO BY
JULIA TURSHEN

Small Victories
Feed the Resistance
Now & Again
Simply Julia

WHAT
GOES
WITH
WHAT

WHAT GOES WITH WHAT

100 Recipes, 20 Charts, Endless Possibilities

JULIA TURSHEN

FLATIRON
BOOKS
NEW YORK

All photographs by Julia Turshen, except the following:

Natalie Chitwood: pages 4, 20, 43, 44–45, 57, 65, 86, 98, 109 (photographs of tools, truck, and sign on shed), 194–95, 205, 300–301, 303, 320

Erin Enouen: page 106

Margo Sivin: pages 258–59

———————————————

WHAT GOES WITH WHAT.
Copyright © 2024 by Julia Turshen. All rights reserved.
Printed in the United States of America.
For information, address Flatiron Books, 120 Broadway, New York, NY 10271.

www.flatironbooks.com

Designed by Doug Turshen with Steve Turner

Library of Congress Cataloging-in-Publication Data

Names: Turshen, Julia, author.
Title: What goes with what : 100 recipes, 20 charts, endless possibilities
  / Julia Turshen.
Description: First edition. | New York : Flatiron Books, [2024] | Includes
  index.
Identifiers: LCCN 2024012028 | ISBN 9781250340962 (paper over board) | ISBN
  9781250340979 (ebook)
Subjects: LCSH: Cooking. | LCGFT: Cookbooks.
Classification: LCC TX714 .T89 2024 | DDC 641.5—dc23/eng/20240327
LC record available at https://lccn.loc.gov/2024012028

Our books may be purchased in bulk for promotional, educational,
or business use. Please contact your local bookseller or the Macmillan
Corporate and Premium Sales Department at 1-800-221-7945,
extension 5442, or by email at MacmillanSpecialMarkets@macmillan.com.

First Edition: 2024

10 9 8 7 6 5 4 3 2 1

For my parents, Rochelle and Doug,
who have taught me that books make your world bigger
and that making them can be so much fun

TABLE OF CONTENTS

Introduction 10
Learned Kitchen Wisdom 14

SECTION ONE: SALADS + SANDWICHES

Salad Dressings 22
Salads with Lettuce 28
Non-Lettuce Salads 40
Sandwiches 54
On Teaching 64

SECTION TWO: VEGETABLES

Stovetop Vegetables 70
Roasted Vegetables 82
Stuffed Vegetables 94
That Time I Was a Farmer 107

SECTION THREE: SOUPS + STEWS + BRAISES

Brothy Soups 112
Pureed Soups 126
Stews 136
Braises 148
For the Love of Better Than Bouillon 160

SECTION FOUR: RICE, MORE GRAINS + PASTA

One-Pot Rice Dishes 164
Grain Bowls 176
Quick Pastas 188
A Conversation with My Mom About Our Bodies 202

SECTION FIVE: MAIN DISHES

Meatballs 208
Sautéed Chicken Dishes 220
Sheet Pan Dinners 232
Savory Pies 244
On Queer Cooking 256

SECTION SIX: BAKED GOODS

One-Bowl Batters 262
Fruity Cobblers + Crisps 276
A Conversation with My Cousin Ivy + My Mom About the Bakery 290

Menu Suggestions 294
Conversion Table 299
Thank You To . . . 302
Index 304
Behind the Scenes 316

INTRODUCTION

Every time I get ready to chop something on my cutting board, I first place a damp paper towel on my counter, which helps keep the board from moving around while I'm working on it. This one simple act sets me up for success in my kitchen. It means I'm starting my work on a sturdy surface, on stable ground. In a way, it's setting an intention, making a gesture to myself that my tools are ready and my kitchen is safe. The moment almost feels like a tiny secular prayer before I start cooking. As vital as this moment is in my kitchen, it's not something I usually mention in my recipes; I think it's a bit of learned wisdom I've come to take for granted. But I thought it was worth mentioning here because my goal in this book is to take nothing for granted. I hope to share all that accumulated knowledge so that you don't leave these pages with just some new recipes to try but also with a deeper understanding of how to really wrap your head around cooking and a way to intuitively understand why certain things go with others.

I think in charts, in frameworks that help connect the dots. What I mean by this is that I think of different types of dishes like big umbrellas that have a basic structure and within these categories, endless combinations are possible. This makes the infiniteness of cooking feel so much more manageable to me. When you see, for example, that all great sandwiches have something crunchy like lettuce, something rich like bacon, something creamy like mayo, and something acidic like tomatoes, you don't just see a BLT—you see a formula for great sandwiches

You see what connects BLTs to Italian combos, tuna melts, Mexican tortas, Cuban sandwiches, bánh mì, and more.

When I cook, I feel relaxed, creative, and confident, in part because after cooking professionally for so many years, I understand how and why things work. I want you to feel the same way, no matter how long you've been cooking. I want the charts I've included to provide education and inspiration. I want them to help you see the big picture so that the small picture feels easier to figure out. I'll be thrilled, of course, if you cook directly from the recipes, but I'll be even more excited if you riff off them and create your own favorite dishes.

While I believe in the scaffolding that recipes provide and appreciate the hard work that goes into well-written and tested recipes, I'm always concerned that they can seem inflexible, like there's only one way to get it "right." Sometimes I think too much detail creates, rather than alleviates, anxiety. "You can actually do anything you want!" I want to shout into my readers' kitchens. "There's no one right way to make anything!" is a magnet I wish I could put on everyone's refrigerator. I've tried to get this idea across in my earlier books and my newsletter and my online cooking classes, but I really think the best way to demonstrate this message is visually, through charts.

I don't think everyone needs to love to cook, or even to cook at all. But if you do want to cook, I think you deserve to feel relaxed about it. Our world and lives are plenty stressful already. Preparing food doesn't have to add to that stress. If you're feeling intimidated by cooking at home, or stuck in a rut, I hope this book unlocks something for you and helps you feel empowered.

A quick note on ingredients, measurements, and serving sizes: The more seasoned I get, the less I care about how exact everything is, and I wish this low-pressure feeling for you too. You'll notice that herbs are measured in handfuls and lots of substitutions are offered throughout (use any color onion, use honey or maple syrup, etc.). You're making dinner, not perfecting a code. Don't worry, though—I haven't avoided all decision-making! While there's built-in flexibility to substitute ingredients where it won't make a difference in the success of the recipe, I've kept these suggestions within a set of trusty parameters. In other words, I've got your back. The goal is to learn to improvise in ways that *work*.

On a similar note, I regularly suggest that you "season to taste," which just means to keep adding salt (and sometimes pepper, other spices, lemon, etc.) until the dish you're making tastes good to you. Whatever that amount is for you is perfect. It might be less than I like or a little more, and that doesn't matter at all, because you're not cooking for me (though I'd be happy to come over anytime!). I think everyone who cooks has a certain intuition about what works and tastes good, and the only way to learn to trust your instincts is to keep cooking and eating what you like to cook. This is also where the charts come in, to help you grow your intuitive sense of

what goes with what. When you understand why something is in a recipe, it's easy to figure out a substitution that can play the same role. Fresh out of lemons? See how a splash of your favorite vinegar works. Allergic to nuts? Try something else rich and crunchy, like toasted pumpkin seeds. Hate cilantro? Then don't use it! You can mix and match. Play. Feel free to . . . feel free. If something doesn't turn out great, remember that it's all part of the learning process (also, contrary to what social media might suggest, not every meal you eat has to be the best meal you've ever had!).

As for serving sizes, making this book has come at a time when I'm continuing to divest myself from diet culture. I hope this is reflected in how I've approached serving sizes (as well as how I talk about food in general). Wherever possible, I've given a total yield (2 quarts of soup, for example) rather than the number of people it will serve. Where that's not possible I've used the word "about" for serving sizes (e.g., "serves about 4"), because I want you to have a sense of how much you're cooking, of course, but I don't believe one serving size fits all. The more you cook, the more you'll have a sense of, for example, things like how far a pound of ground meat goes in your household and whether you consider a chopped salad a meal or part of a meal.

Again, there are no rules. There's you in your kitchen and me in mine, offering as much support as I can. If you don't already trust yourself in your kitchen, I think you will soon. Please know that I already do.

Here I am with all the charts! I could barely feel my right hand at this point, but I was (and am!) so happy. . . .

LEARNED KITCHEN WISDOM

PLACE A DAMP PAPER TOWEL
UNDER YOUR CUTTING BOARD.
IT WILL KEEP YOUR BOARD SECURE!

COAT MEASURING CUPS WITH NONSTICK SPRAY BEFORE MEASURING STICKY INGREDIENTS!

BEFORE CLOSING THEM, WIPE THE EDGES OF STICKY JARS WITH A TOWEL YOU'VE DAMPENED WITH HOT WATER TO KEEP THE LID FROM STICKING TO THE JAR.

BUY OLIVE OIL
IN BULK &
DECANT INTO
A SQUEEZE
BOTTLE — EASIER
TO POUR & CHEAPER!

IF FREEZING
SOMETHING LIQUIDY,
LEAVE ENOUGH
ROOM AT THE TOP
OF YOUR CONTAINER
TO ALLOW FOR FOOD
TO EXPAND.

USE MASKING TAPE FOR EVERYTHING IN YOUR PANTRY, ESPECIALLY FOR REMINDING YOURSELF OF YOUR MOST USED MEASUREMENTS.

AN IMMERSION BLENDER is <u>SO</u> UNDERRATED— LESS TO CLEAN, LESS HASSLE, LESS $!

GRATE GARLIC OR GINGER ON A MICROPLANE BEFORE INCORPORATING INTO A SALAD DRESSING OR A SAUCE.

BRING YOUR POT OF WATER TO A BOIL BEFORE YOU THINK YOU NEED IT, GET YOUR GRILL GOING EARLY, PREHEAT YOUR OVEN — LET THESE THINGS WAIT FOR YOU, NOT THE OTHER WAY AROUND!

SMALL OFFSET SPATULAS ARE SO USEFUL! USE ONE TO FROST A CAKE OR TO SPREAD MAYO ON A SANDWICH. USE TWO TO FLIP LATKES, FRITTERS, OR PANCAKES!

MAKE YOUR LIFE
EASIER BY
EMBRACING
INGREDIENTS THAT
OFFER LOTS OF
BUILT-IN FLAVOR—
KIMCHI, TOMATO
PASTE, PICKLES, ETC.

THE MORE YOU COOK, THE MORE YOU KNOW. ♡

SECTION ONE:
SALADS & SANDWICHES

SALAD DRESSINGS

There's a whole world of salad dressings, from the simplest pour of olive oil and squeeze of lemon directly onto your salad, no whisking or measuring involved, to the most complex, the blended types with multiple ingredients (like Caesar). My basic formula for dressing is one part something acidic, two to three parts fat, plus seasoning. That's it! Acid can be anything from lemon to vinegar; fat can be anything from oil to yogurt. Seasoning can be as simple as salt, as layered as several fresh herbs plus garlic and honey. You can combine everything in a jar and shake it, whisk the ingredients together a bowl, or use a blender.

SALAD DRESSINGS	ACID (1 PART)	FAT (2-3 PARTS)	SEASONING
CREAMY LEMON DRESSING	FRESH LEMON ZEST & JUICE	50/50 OLIVE OIL + GREEK YOGURT	HONEY + SALT
PIZZERIA VINAIGRETTE	RED WINE VINEGAR	OLIVE OIL	DRIED OREGANO, GARLIC & SALT
CREAMY MUSTARD DRESSING	WHITE WINE VINEGAR	EQUAL PARTS OLIVE OIL + MAYO	DIJON, HONEY, SALT + PEPPER
KIMCHI DRESSING	KIMCHI JUICE & RICE VINEGAR	MAYO	SOY SAUCE, FISH SAUCE, SALT & KOREAN RED PEPPER FLAKES
TAHINI RANCH DRESSING	RED WINE VINEGAR	TAHINI + BOILING WATER, PLUS MAYO	HONEY, GARLIC, SALT, FRESH CHIVES & DILL

CREAMY LEMON DRESSING

I can't think of many dishes that wouldn't be improved by a drizzle of this dressing, full of bright lemon zest and juice (it's even great for pasta salads!). If dairy is not your thing, you can substitute coconut yogurt or vegan mayonnaise for regular yogurt.

Makes about ⅔ cup

1 lemon

¼ cup extra-virgin olive oil

¼ cup full-fat plain yogurt

2 teaspoons honey (or maple syrup)

½ teaspoon kosher salt

Use a Microplane or similar tool to finely grate the zest of the lemon. Place the zest in a bowl. Halve the lemon, squeeze the juice from it, and add it to the zest. Add the olive oil, yogurt, honey, and salt and whisk well to combine (or blend everything in the pitcher of a blender, or combine everything in a jar, screw on the lid, and shake vigorously, then store in the jar). Store for up to a week in a covered container (or jar) in the refrigerator.

PIZZERIA VINAIGRETTE

This is probably the dressing I make most often. It's as good on a bowl of chopped romaine as it is drizzled over a platter of roasted peppers. Try it on your next sandwich, or use it as a sauce for grilled steak. If your vinaigrette turns solid in the refrigerator, just let it sit at room temperature until the oil goes back to being liquid (or microwave it for 10 seconds, stir, and repeat if needed).

Makes about ½ cup

⅓ cup extra-virgin olive oil

3 tablespoons red wine vinegar

½ teaspoon kosher salt

½ teaspoon dried oregano

1 small garlic clove, minced

Place all of the ingredients in a bowl and whisk well to combine (or combine everything in a jar, screw on the lid, and shake vigorously, then store in the jar). Store for up to a week in a covered container (or jar) in the refrigerator.

CREAMY
MUSTARD
DRESSING

PIZZERIA
VINAIGRETTE

TAHINI
RANCH

CREAMY
LEMON
DRESSING

KIMCHI
DRESSING

CREAMY MUSTARD DRESSING

This dressing is particularly excellent on anything hearty (grain salads, lentils, roasted squash, etc.). If you want a bit more mustard *pop!*, whisk in a tablespoon of seeded mustard.

Makes nearly a cup

¼ cup olive oil

¼ cup mayonnaise (regular or vegan)

¼ cup white wine vinegar

2 tablespoons Dijon mustard

1 teaspoon honey (or maple syrup)

Kosher salt and freshly ground black pepper to taste

Place all the ingredients in a bowl and whisk well to combine (or combine everything in a jar, screw on the lid, and shake vigorously, then store in the jar). Store for up to a week in a covered container (or jar) in the refrigerator.

Pro tip for measuring creamy ingredients like mayonnaise that like to stick to the measuring cup: if you're using these in a recipe with any type of liquid, measure that liquid out into a liquid measuring cup, then add as much of the creamy thing to raise the line to the amount you need. For example, in this recipe, I put ¼ cup olive oil in the measuring cup, then added enough mayonnaise so that the mixture comes up to ½ cup, indicating that I have measured out exactly ¼ cup mayonnaise (what I need for the dressing). This is all easier than it might sound—just take a look at the photo!

KIMCHI DRESSING

The juice from a jar of kimchi is just as valuable as the kimchi itself. Acidic and packed with flavor, it makes an excellent salad dressing ingredient (if you don't have ½ cup from your jar, add an extra splash of rice vinegar and an extra pinch of red pepper flakes). Use this dressing on sliced avocados, chopped cucumber salad, or coleslaw. It's also fantastic spooned over a bowl of rice and eggs or as a marinade for chicken or pork. If you've never used Korean red pepper flakes (widely available at Asian grocery stores and places like Whole Foods), they're worth seeking out—they're not that spicy and they add so much flavor.

Makes about 1¼ cups

½ cup juice from a jar of kimchi

½ cup mayonnaise (regular or vegan)

1 tablespoon unseasoned rice vinegar

2 teaspoons soy sauce

2 teaspoons fish sauce (or additional soy sauce)

½ teaspoon kosher salt

1 teaspoon Korean red pepper flakes (or other red pepper flakes, like Turkish silk or Aleppo, or freshly ground black pepper)

Place all the ingredients in a bowl and whisk well to combine (or combine everything in a jar, screw on the lid, and shake vigorously, then store in the jar). Store for up to a week in a covered container (or jar) in the refrigerator.

TAHINI RANCH DRESSING

Tahini's creaminess makes this ranch dressing extra rich. Haley, who moderates the chat in my online cooking classes and tested every single recipe in this book (!), uses this on potato salad, which I think is brilliant (add the dressing to 2½ pounds boiled and halved baby Yukon Gold potatoes, 4 chopped hard-boiled eggs, and a bunch of thinly sliced scallions). It's also fantastic drizzled over a platter of sliced ripe tomatoes.

Makes nearly 2 cups

½ cup well-stirred tahini

½ cup boiling water

⅓ cup red wine vinegar

¼ cup mayonnaise (regular or vegan)

1 tablespoon honey (or maple syrup)

2 garlic cloves, minced

2 teaspoons garlic powder

1 teaspoon kosher salt

A small handful of fresh chives, finely chopped

A small handful of fresh dill, finely chopped

Place all the ingredients in a bowl and whisk well to combine (or blend in the pitcher of a blender, or combine using an immersion blender in a large jar). Store for up to a week in a covered container (or jar) in the refrigerator.

SALADS WITH LETTUCE

For lettuce-based salads, I often start with something crisp (because that's my preference), but use whatever lettuce or leafy green you'd like. Then I like to introduce texture with something crunchy and add something rich to give the salad more substance. Last but not least, finish off with a dressing that complements all the flavors in the salad bowl. I think salad dressing selection is a lot like having the right jacket for the weather—while another might do, having the one you really need for the context makes a big difference.

SALADS WITH LETTUCE	BASE	CRUNCHY THING	RICH THING	DRESSING
CLASSIC CAESAR WITH BIG CRUNCHY CROUTONS	ROMAINE	CROUTONS	SHAVED PARM	Julia's CAESAR
VEGAN KALE CAESAR WITH CRISPY CHICKPEAS	SHREDDED KALE MASSAGED WITH LEMON + SALT	ROASTED CHICKPEAS	EXTRA DRESSING!	CAPER CAESAR
ITALIAN CHOPPED SALAD	CHOPPED ROMAINE, JARRED ARTICHOKE HEARTS + ROASTED PEPPERS	THINLY SLICED PEPPERONCINI	OLIVES, DICED SALAMI & CHEESE	PIZZERIA VINAIGRETTE
WINTER CHOPPED SALAD	SHREDDED KALE & CABBAGE	PUMPKIN SEEDS + PICKLED RED ONIONS	ROASTED SQUASH & CRUMBLED FETA	GO-TO DRESSING
MY USUAL CHOPPED SALAD	CHOPPED ROMAINE & RED CABBAGE	ROASTED ALMONDS + GRATED CARROTS	CHICKPEAS, FETA & GOLDEN RAISINS	CREAMY MUSTARD DRESSING

CLASSIC CAESAR WITH BIG CRUNCHY CROUTONS

I offered a recipe for Caesar dressing in *Small Victories*, my first solo cookbook, called Julia's Caesar. It's my favorite dressing of all time, and the name still makes me laugh. This recipe is built on that one and includes what I've learned since I wrote that book, including the fact that a larger batch is better for so many reasons. First and foremost, it blends more easily. Second, you can use the whole tin of anchovies, oil and all, which is great because then you don't have to figure out what to do with leftover anchovies and anchovy oil. Last, it leaves you with extra dressing, which can be stored in the refrigerator for up to 10 days, and who doesn't want extra Caesar dressing?

Serves about 4

For the dressing (makes 2 cups):

2 large garlic cloves

One 2-ounce tin olive oil–packed anchovy fillets (don't drain—you want to use the oil!)

3 tablespoons fresh lemon juice

3 tablespoons red wine vinegar

3 tablespoons water

⅓ cup mayonnaise

¾ cup extra-virgin olive oil

½ teaspoon kosher salt

½ teaspoon freshly ground black pepper

¾ cup finely grated Parmesan cheese

For the croutons:

3 tablespoons extra-virgin olive oil, plus more if needed

½ pound sourdough, French or Italian, peasant, or country bread (or just about any plain bread), torn into bite-sized pieces

½ teaspoon garlic powder

½ teaspoon kosher salt

For the salad:

3 hearts romaine lettuce, leaves separated, large leaves torn in half

Extra grated Parmesan

First, make the dressing: Place all the ingredients in the pitcher of a blender and puree until smooth. Season the dressing to taste with more salt and/or pepper if needed.

Next, make the croutons: Heat the olive oil in the largest nonstick skillet you have over high heat. Once it starts to shimmer, add the torn bread and toss to combine. If the bread is looking dry, add a little bit more oil. Sprinkle with the garlic powder and salt and cook, tossing now and then, until the bread cubes are browned and starting to crisp, just a few minutes. Transfer the croutons to a plate and set aside to cool (they will crisp up as they cool).

Finish the salad: Place the lettuce in a large salad bowl (or just any big bowl) and drizzle with ½ cup of the dressing. Use your hands or tongs to mix the salad well. Transfer to a serving platter (or just serve from the bowl). Top the salad with the croutons and extra grated Parmesan, and drizzle with a little more dressing. Serve immediately.

VEGAN KALE CAESAR WITH CRISPY CHICKPEAS

Briny, salty capers take the place of anchovies, and nutritional yeast adds all the umami cheesiness of Parmesan in this great vegan Caesar. You'll end up with about 1½ cups of dressing, so you'll have some left over. Use it for other salads or as a dip for cut-up vegetables or potato chips. If you don't have a blender, use a food processor, and if you don't have either one, finely mince the garlic and capers together on your cutting board, scrape into a bowl, and then whisk in everything else (it won't be supersmooth, but just call it "Rustic Caesar" and you'll be fine). If you have an air fryer, cook the chickpeas in that (375°F for 12 to 15 minutes, shaking the basket halfway through). You can also swap croutons for the chickpeas.

Serves about 4

For the chickpeas:
One 15-ounce can chickpeas, drained and rinsed

2 tablespoons extra-virgin olive oil

½ teaspoon kosher salt

½ teaspoon garlic powder

½ teaspoon sweet paprika

For the dressing:
2 large garlic cloves

One 3.5-ounce jar capers (including the brine!)

2 tablespoons red wine vinegar

2 tablespoons fresh lemon juice

½ cup vegan mayonnaise

½ cup extra-virgin olive oil

½ teaspoon kosher salt

½ teaspoon freshly ground black pepper

3 tablespoons nutritional yeast

For the salad:
1 bunch (1 pound) kale (curly or lacinato), tough stems removed, roughly chopped

Half a lemon

A large pinch of kosher salt

First, prepare the chickpeas: Preheat your oven to 425°F.

Place a paper towel on a sheet pan, put the chickpeas on top of it, and roll them around a bit to dry them off. Remove the paper towel and drizzle the chickpeas with the oil. Sprinkle with the salt, garlic powder, and paprika and use your hands to mix everything well. Roast, shaking the pan once or twice during cooking, until the chickpeas are browned and crispy, about 20 minutes. Remove from the oven and set aside to cool before using (they will crisp as they cool).

Next, make the dressing: Place all the dressing ingredients in the pitcher of a blender and puree until smooth. Season the dressing to taste with more salt and/or pepper if needed.

Finish the salad: Place the kale in a large bowl and squeeze the juice from the lemon half over it. Sprinkle with the salt and use your hands to scrunch it all together. Really get in there—don't be shy! This will help make the kale easier to eat. Drizzle with ½ cup of the dressing and use your hands or tongs to mix the salad well. Transfer to a serving platter (or just serve from the bowl).

Top the salad with the chickpeas and drizzle with another ⅓ cup or so of the dressing. Serve immediately.

ITALIAN CHOPPED SALAD

Tied with Caesar for my favorite salad, this is a testament to the ease and flavor of using a bunch of jars of preserved ingredients. Pro tip: before you slice the pepperoncini peppers, split them open over the salad bowl so that the brine inside them ends up in your dressing, not on your cutting board (or just buy sliced pepperoncini and don't worry about the brine!).

Serves about 4

1 batch Pizzeria Vinaigrette (page 24)

3 hearts romaine lettuce, chopped into 1-inch pieces

One 6-ounce jar marinated artichoke hearts, drained and roughly chopped

One 6-ounce jar roasted red peppers, drained and roughly chopped

A large handful of pitted olives (any type you like), roughly chopped

6 jarred pepperoncini peppers, stems discarded, thinly sliced

¼ pound thinly sliced provolone cheese, diced

¼ pound thinly sliced Genoa salami, diced

Place the Pizzeria Vinaigrette in the bottom of your bowl (if you haven't made it yet, just whisk all the ingredients together in the bowl you're going to mix the salad in). Add the remaining ingredients and stir well to combine. Serve immediately.

A few notes here: The dressing is the Go-To Dressing from *Simply Julia*, which is just equal parts olive oil, apple cider vinegar, tahini, and soy sauce (it's SO GOOD). The pickled red onions are great to make a day or even up to two weeks ahead and have in a jar in the fridge (you could also use store-bought pickled onions). Lastly, if you have an air fryer, use it for the squash (400°F for 15 minutes; shake the basket halfway through cooking).

Serves about 4

For the pickled red onions:
1 red onion, thinly sliced

1 garlic clove, thinly sliced

½ cup white vinegar

½ cup water

2 teaspoons sugar

1½ teaspoons kosher salt

For the roasted squash:
One 12-ounce package frozen butternut squash (or 1 medium butternut squash, peeled, seeded, and cut into 1-inch pieces)

2 tablespoons olive oil

Kosher salt and freshly ground black pepper

For the dressing:
2 tablespoons extra-virgin olive oil

2 tablespoons apple cider vinegar

2 tablespoons well-stirred tahini

2 tablespoons soy sauce

For the base of the salad:
½ pound kale (curly or lacinato), tough stems removed, finely shredded

½ pound green cabbage, finely shredded

Half a lemon

Kosher salt and freshly ground black pepper

For the rest of the salad:
¼ pound feta, crumbled (about 1 cup)

½ cup roasted pumpkin seeds (salted or unsalted, up to you)

Prepare the pickled red onions: Place all the ingredients in a pint jar and screw the lid on tightly. Shake until the salt and sugar dissolve. Use straightaway, or store in the refrigerator for up to 2 weeks.

Roast the squash: Preheat your oven to 425°F. Place the squash on a sheet pan, drizzle with the olive oil, sprinkle with a large pinch of salt and a few grinds of black pepper, and toss well. Roast, stirring occasionally, until the squash is just tender and beginning to brown, about 25 minutes. Remove from the oven.

While the squash is roasting, make the dressing: Place all the dressing ingredients in a small bowl and whisk well to combine.

Prepare the salad base: Place the kale and cabbage in a large serving or salad bowl and squeeze the juice from the lemon half over the greens. Sprinkle with a large pinch of salt and a few grinds of black pepper and use your hands to scrunch everything all together. Really get in there—don't be shy! This will help make the kale and cabbage easier to eat.

Finish the salad: Place the roasted squash on top of the kale and cabbage, scatter the feta and pumpkin seeds on the squash, and drizzle with the dressing. Add as many of the pickled onions as you'd like (get them out of the jar with a fork, so you leave the brine behind). Mix well to combine and serve immediately.

MY USUAL CHOPPED SALAD

I have this salad for lunch at least once a week, sometimes with some leftover grilled or roasted chicken mixed in, sometimes with a hard-boiled egg sliced on top, sometimes with half a diced avocado stirred in. Occasionally I buy "smokehouse" flavored almonds and use those instead of the regular roasted ones. Go nuts!

Serves about 4

2 hearts romaine lettuce, chopped into 1-inch pieces

½ pound red cabbage, finely chopped

2 carrots, coarsely grated

One 15-ounce can chickpeas, drained and rinsed

½ cup roasted almonds, roughly chopped (salted or unsalted, up to you)

½ cup golden raisins

¼ pound feta, crumbled (about 1 cup)

½ cup Creamy Mustard Dressing (page 26) or your favorite vinaigrette

Place everything in a large serving or salad bowl and mix well to combine. Serve immediately.

NON-LETTUCE SALADS

I apply the same formula to non-lettuce salads as I do to lettuce-based ones: base + crunchy thing + rich thing + dressing. The only variable that really changes is the base, which can be just about anything beyond lettuce. I'm talking grain salads, bean salads, tomato salads, avocado salads, cucumber salads, potato salads, and more. Then just add crunch, richness, and dressing for a delicious and memorable salad.

NON-LETTUCE SALADS	BASE	CRUNCHY THING	RICH THING	DRESSING
CUCUMBER + AVOCADO SALAD	SLICED CUCUMBERS	CHOPPED CABBAGE KIMCHI	DICED AVOCADO	KIMCHI JUICE & MAYO
SHAVED FENNEL + APPLE SALAD	SHAVED FENNEL & APPLES	TOASTED NUTS	SALTY CHEESE	OLIVE OIL, LEMON & HONEY
FARRO & ROASTED VEGETABLE SALAD	COOKED FARRO & ROASTED VEG.	TOASTED NUTS	CRUMBLED CHEESE	CREAMY MUSTARD DRESSING
A GREAT CARROT SALAD	THINLY SLICED CARROTS	ROASTED ALMONDS	CASTELVETRANO OLIVES & GOLDEN RAISINS	OLIVE OIL, LEMON & HONEY
ROASTED BROCCOLI + PEANUT SALAD	ROASTED BROCCOLI	TOASTED PEANUTS & THINLY SLICED SCALLIONS	BACON	EASY PEANUT DRESSING

CUCUMBER + AVOCADO SALAD

Cabbage kimchi adds two-for-one flavor to this salad, first as a chopped crunchy ingredient and second as the base of the dressing. You can turn this into a bigger salad by adding chopped lettuce (something crunchy, like romaine, is great) and more dressing, plus things like thinly sliced or grated carrots, cooked broccoli, radishes, tomatoes . . . basically, anything! This is a great side dish with the Spicy Chicken with Lime + Cashews (page 228), but it can really be served with whatever needs some extra green and crunch.

Serves about 4 as a side dish

1 English cucumber (or ¾ pound any type of cucumber), thinly sliced

1 large ripe avocado, halved, pitted, and diced

½ cup drained cabbage kimchi, finely chopped, plus 3 tablespoons juice from the kimchi jar

3 tablespoons mayonnaise (regular or vegan)

Kosher salt

Korean red pepper flakes (or freshly ground black pepper)

Place the cucumber, avocado, and chopped kimchi on a serving platter (I like to do it in that order, the cucumber acting as a bed for the avocado and the kimchi acting almost like sprinkles). Place the kimchi juice and mayonnaise in a small bowl, whisk together, and season to taste with salt and red pepper flakes. Drizzle the dressing evenly over the salad and serve immediately.

Two quick pro tips about avocado safety: please put your avocado half on your cutting board (rather than in your hand!) before whacking your knife in the pit to remove it (what if you miss the pit!?); also, once you've removed the pit and it's stuck on your knife, just pinch above the pit and it will drop right off.

You absolutely do not need
to harvest the fennel
yourself to make the Shaved
Fennel + Apple Salad
on the next page, but I
just love to be extra. . . .

SHAVED FENNEL + APPLE SALAD

I love this beautiful slaw-like salad for holiday dinners because its brightness complements richer dishes (roasted chicken or turkey, salmon, and steak all come to mind), plus it holds up well (couldn't we all use more things that hold up well?). If you don't like fennel, try another firm vegetable like kohlrabi or celery. You can also swap firm pears for the apple, or opt for peeled and sliced citrus. To make this more substantial, you could mix in any type of cooked grain.

Serves about 4 as a side dish

¼ cup extra-virgin olive oil

2 tablespoons fresh lemon juice

1 teaspoon honey (or maple syrup)

½ teaspoon kosher salt

1 large head fennel, any browned outer layers removed

1 large apple (any kind, but preferably tart), cored, thinly sliced

½ cup toasted nuts, roughly chopped if you'd like

½ cup shaved Parmesan (or any firm salty cheese)

Place the olive oil, lemon juice, honey, and salt in a large bowl and whisk well to combine.

If your fennel has fronds and long stalks attached, separate them, roughly chop the fronds, and thinly slice the stalks (as if each were a celery stalk) using either a mandoline if you're comfortable using one or just a sharp knife. Thinly slice the fennel bulb (with a mandoline or a sharp knife). Add all your fennel to the bowl, along with the apple, nuts, and cheese, and gently toss everything together to combine (your hands are a great tool for this). Serve immediately, or set aside/refrigerate until ready to serve. The salad can be kept at room temperature for up to a couple of hours or stored covered in the refrigerator for up to a few days; serve at room temperature.

FARRO + ROASTED VEGETABLE SALAD

This is an infinitely versatile recipe. Any grain can be used instead of farro, and just about any type of roasted vegetable works. Same goes for the nuts, cheese, and herbs. Have fun with your combinations, and use this salad as an excuse to clear out your fridge! If you'd like to add more flavor to the farro, cook it in vegetable or chicken broth instead of salted water (or just add some Better Than Bouillon to the water).

Serves about 4 as a side dish

2 pounds root vegetables (I like a mix of carrots, parsnips, and turnips, but use whatever you'd like), peeled as needed, cut into bite-sized pieces

¼ cup olive oil

Kosher salt and freshly ground black pepper

1 cup farro

¼ cup Creamy Mustard Dressing (page 26) or your favorite vinaigrette

A small handful (about ¼ cup) toasted nuts (such as walnuts, hazelnuts, pistachios, or almonds; if you can't do nuts, use pumpkin or sunflower seeds)

A small handful (about ¼ cup) crumbled cheese (goat, feta, Manchego, cheddar . . . this is flexible!)

A handful of chopped fresh herbs (parsley, dill, chives . . . whatever you've got), if you'd like

Preheat your oven to 425°F.

Place the root vegetables on a sheet pan. Drizzle with the olive oil, sprinkle with a big pinch of salt, and grind over a bit of black pepper. Toss everything well to coat and then spread the vegetables out in an even layer. Roast the vegetables, stirring them now and then, until softened, browned, and crisp on the edges, about 30 minutes.

Meanwhile, bring a large pot of water to a boil and season it generously with salt. Add the farro and cook, stirring now and then, until tender, about 30 minutes. Drain the farro in a colander and place in a serving bowl.

Add half the dressing to the farro while it's still warm and stir well to combine. Season to taste with more salt if needed.

Add the roasted vegetables to the farro and stir gently to combine. Top with the nuts and cheese and drizzle with the remaining dressing. Sprinkle with the herbs, if using. Serve warm or at room temperature.

A GREAT CARROT SALAD

I adore carrots. They keep for so long in the fridge, they're inexpensive, and they can go in just about any dish. And because they're so familiar, I think they have a great capacity to surprise you when you treat them with a little elegance. Thinly slicing them and combining them with sweet raisins, buttery olives, and rich almonds is one of my favorite ways to do that. Serve this salad with any number of things—a bowl of hummus, a pot of rice, and a pile of greens for a delicious vegan meal, or alongside grilled sausages and mashed potatoes for something a bit heartier. Really it's like a great pair of jeans that can go with anything (this is all the fashion advice I can offer).

Serves about 4 as a side dish

¼ cup extra-virgin olive oil

2 tablespoons fresh lemon juice

1 teaspoon honey (or maple syrup)

½ teaspoon kosher salt

4 large carrots (¾ to 1 pound), peeled, sliced into thin coins (or coarsely grated)

A large handful of fresh flat-leaf parsley (or any soft green herb), roughly chopped

⅓ cup golden raisins

⅔ cup pitted green olives, preferably Castelvetrano, roughly chopped

⅓ cup roasted almonds (salted or not, up to you!), roughly chopped

Place the olive oil, lemon juice, honey, and salt in a large bowl and whisk well to combine. Add the remaining ingredients, stir well to combine, and serve immediately.

ROASTED BROCCOLI + PEANUT SALAD

If you know someone who is hesitant to eat broccoli, please make this salad for them and see what happens. And if you do not eat bacon, just leave it out! Otherwise, cook the bacon however you like (in a skillet, in the microwave or air fryer, or even on a sheet pan in the oven—and then use that same sheet pan for the broccoli). No need to drain the bacon fat; just use it instead of the olive oil. Brussels sprouts or green beans can easily be swapped for the broccoli (both are substantial, can hold up to roasting, and will get similarly sweet). If you're making this for someone with a peanut allergy, any nut or seed butter can be used in place of the peanut butter (and then use that same nut or seed in place of the whole peanuts). All these alternatives are a great reminder that when you know the purpose of an ingredient in a recipe, it's easy to feel confident about switching things up.

Serves about 4 as a side dish

2 pounds broccoli, tough stems discarded, cut into large florets

¼ cup olive oil

Kosher salt

¼ cup creamy peanut butter (you can eyeball the amount, as measuring peanut butter is a sticky business)

¼ cup boiling water

2 tablespoons unseasoned rice vinegar

1 teaspoon soy sauce

1 teaspoon honey (or maple syrup)

Freshly ground black pepper

4 slices bacon (about ¼ pound), cooked and crumbled

¼ cup salted roasted peanuts, roughly chopped

2 scallions, ends trimmed, thinly sliced

Preheat your oven to 425°F.

Place the broccoli on a sheet pan, drizzle with the olive oil, and sprinkle with a big pinch of salt. Toss everything well to combine and then spread the broccoli out in an even layer. Roast the broccoli, stirring it now and then, until softened, browned, and crisp on the edges, about 25 minutes.

While the broccoli roasts, make the dressing: Place the peanut butter in a bowl, add the boiling water, rice vinegar, soy sauce, and honey, and whisk well until smooth (at first it will look a bit of a mess, but it comes together beautifully after vigorous whisking). Season to taste with salt and pepper.

When the broccoli is cooked, transfer it to a serving platter. Drizzle evenly with the dressing and top with the bacon, peanuts, and scallions. Serve warm or at room temperature.

SANDWICHES

Do you need my guidance on how to make a sandwich? Probably not. But understanding the components of a single great sandwich unlocks the formula of all great sandwiches. Remember the BLT, which I highlighted in the introduction (page 10). It's bread plus a main thing (bacon), plus a creamy layer (mayo), something crunchy (lettuce!), and an extra acidic thing (a well-seasoned ripe tomato). Using this formula means making a great sandwich every time you make one. Here are my top five.

SANDWICH	BREAD
BLT	LIGHTLY TOASTED WHITE
A GREAT TUNA SANDWICH	LIGHTLY TOASTED PUMPER-NICKEL
COLD ROAST CHICKEN SANDWICH	LIGHTLY TOASTED RYE
MY FAVORITE VEGGIE SANDWICH	LIGHTLY TOASTED WHOLE WHEAT
BEST HAM SANDWICH	GRAINY SANDWICH BREAD

MAIN THING	CREAMY LAYER	CRUNCHY LAYER	EXTRA ACIDIC THING
BACON	MAYO	LETTUCE	RIPE TOMATO WITH LOTS OF S & P
GREAT TUNA SALAD	BUILT INTO THE TUNA SALAD	SHREDDED ICEBERG & POTATO CHIPS	SLICED BANANA PEPPERS
COLD ROAST CHICKEN	RUSSIAN DRESSING	LETTUCE	PICKLED PEPPERS
SLICED CHEDDAR	HUMMUS	CUCUMBER	GRATED CARROTS WITH OIL & VINEGAR
SLICED HAM & CHEDDAR	GARLICKY MAYO	LETTUCE	CREAMY MUSTARD DRESSING

BLT

To make my BLT-loving life easier, I cook bacon in my air fryer (I line the basket with parchment for easy cleanup and do 350°F for 8 minutes).

Makes 1 sandwich (easily multiplied)

2 slices white sandwich bread, lightly toasted

Mayonnaise (as much as you like)

2 thick or 4 regular slices bacon, cooked until crisp

A couple of crunchy iceberg lettuce leaves

A few thick slices of a very ripe tomato

Kosher salt and freshly ground black pepper

Spread one side of each piece of bread with as much mayonnaise as you'd like (I like a lot). Layer the bacon and lettuce on top of one slice. Top with the tomatoes, seasoning each tomato slice generously with salt and pepper as you add it. Close the sandwich and enjoy immediately.

A GREAT TUNA SANDWICH

A simple tuna salad plus shredded iceberg, banana peppers, and potato chips means tuna sandwich heaven. So much crunch! This sandwich is an overstuffed mess, in the best way. If you're looking for a smaller bite, though, you can split the tuna salad between two sandwiches.

Makes 1 large sandwich (easily multiplied)

For the tuna salad:

One 5-ounce can solid white tuna, drained

3 tablespoons mayonnaise

1 tablespoon Dijon mustard

Juice of half a lemon

1 celery stalk, very finely chopped

Kosher salt and freshly ground black pepper

For the sandwich:

2 slices pumpernickel bread, lightly toasted

A handful of shredded iceberg lettuce

About 2 tablespoons sliced banana peppers (or pepperoncini peppers), drained

A small handful of potato chips

Make the tuna salad: Place the tuna, mayonnaise, mustard, lemon juice, and celery in a bowl and season generously with salt and pepper. Stir until combined.

Assemble the sandwich: Spoon half the tuna salad onto each slice of bread. Top one slice with the lettuce, banana peppers, and potato chips. Place the other slice on top (so the lettuce, peppers, and chips will be between tuna!) and gently press down to crunch the chips into the tuna. Enjoy immediately with plenty of napkins!

MY FAVORITE VEGGIE SANDWICH

Grated carrots dressed with oil and vinegar make a crunchy, juicy layer in this sandwich, almost like a slaw. They're a fun thing to add to any sandwich to give it an unexpected acidic punch, whether it's a simple turkey, mayo, and cheese situation on a roll, or something a little fancier, like thinly sliced roast beef with horseradish aioli (by "fancy," I mean using the word "aioli" to describe mayonnaise mixed with prepared horseradish).

Makes 1 sandwich (easily multiplied)

1 carrot, coarsely grated

1½ teaspoons olive oil

1½ teaspoons balsamic vinegar (or any vinegar)

A large pinch of salt plus a little freshly ground black pepper

2 slices whole wheat sandwich bread, lightly toasted

¼ cup creamy hummus (store-bought or homemade)

About 2 ounces sharp cheddar cheese, thinly sliced

A few thin cucumber slices

Place the grated carrot, olive oil, vinegar, salt, and pepper in a small bowl and stir well to combine. Spread one side of each piece of bread with 2 tablespoons of the hummus and then layer the cheese, cucumber, and marinated carrots on one slice. Close the sandwich with the other slice of bread (hummus side down!). Cut in half and eat immediately, or wrap it up, take it with you, and eat whenever.

COLD ROAST CHICKEN SANDWICH

For my dad, the whole point of roasting a chicken is to have leftovers for sandwiches the next day. Slicing it cold and layering it on rye bread with Russian dressing is just classic Doug Turshen, and I can't recommend the combination highly enough. The cherry peppers are my addition (can't help myself!), and they add that special something.

Makes 1 sandwich (easily multiplied)

1½ tablespoons mayonnaise

1½ tablespoons ketchup

Kosher salt and freshly ground black pepper

2 slices seeded rye bread, lightly toasted

Half a leftover cold roasted chicken breast, thinly sliced

A couple of butter lettuce leaves

A few sweet pickled cherry peppers, drained and sliced (or a sliced dill pickle)

Place the mayonnaise and ketchup in a small bowl and season generously with salt and pepper. Stir the mixture together and then divide it between the two slices of bread and spread it evenly so it completely covers each piece of bread. Layer the chicken, lettuce, and sliced cherry peppers on one slice. Close the sandwich with the other slice of bread (Russian dressing side down, obviously). Cut in half and eat immediately.

BEST HAM SANDWICH

Dressing the lettuce before adding it to a sandwich is a tiny bit of extra effort that pays off big-time. Same with adding a little minced garlic to your mayo. I could eat this sandwich every day, and when we have sliced ham in our house, I do.

Makes 1 sandwich (easily multiplied)

3 tablespoons mayonnaise

½ garlic clove, minced

Kosher salt and freshly ground black pepper

2 slices grainy sandwich bread (not toasted)

2 or 3 slices Black Forest ham

A few thin slices sharp cheddar cheese

1 large romaine lettuce leaf, torn in half

2 teaspoons Creamy Mustard Dressing (page 26) or your favorite vinaigrette

Place the mayonnaise and garlic in a small bowl and season generously with salt and pepper. Stir the mixture together and then divide it between the two slices of bread, spreading it out so it completely covers the bread. Layer the ham and cheese on one slice of bread.

Place the lettuce on a plate (or just on your cutting board) and drizzle with the dressing. Use your hands to coat the lettuce with the dressing, then add it to the sandwich. Close the sandwich with the other slice of bread (mayo side down, clearly). Cut in half and eat immediately.

ON TEACHING

When my last cookbook, *Simply Julia*, came out in early 2021, all my book events and promotion took place online. This was because the coronavirus pandemic changed the way book publishers toured authors, but the happy result was that rather than traveling and doing cooking demonstrations in kitchens I had never stepped foot in, I could do everything from my own kitchen, the place I am most comfortable in the whole world. It also meant anyone watching was welcome to cook along with me in their own kitchen, rather than just sit and watch me in a public setting. Whereas I used to avoid cooking demos because they made me anxious—everyone just *watching me cook!*—pivoting to doing them online let me actually love the process. I enjoyed it all so much that I started offering online cooking classes after my book promotion was finished. I now teach on Zoom most Sunday afternoons, and it's become a huge part of my work and something I look forward to.

People join from across the country, and from other countries as well, and no matter how many classes I teach, it never gets old to me that there are so many of us in so many different places but we're all choosing to be together at the same time making the same things. I've written before about the feeling of solidarity I have with other home cooks when I'm cooking by myself, the warmth I feel when I pause and remind myself that people across the world are doing some version of what I'm doing in that moment. My online classes are a visceral reminder of how connected we can feel even when we are far apart.

What I love most about the classes are the people I interact with. First there's Haley Scarpino, who moderates the chat. Before I started teaching regularly, my spouse, Grace,

would help me by keeping an eye on the chat and letting me know if anyone had questions (this way, I didn't have to try to be in two places at once or try to type with messy hands). When I decided to make my classes a regular thing, Grace compassionately suggested I find someone permanent for the job. From the moment I first spoke to Haley, I knew she'd be amazing. I like to think of my classes as opening my kitchen to a bunch of people for a cooking party. Haley is the friend who makes sure everyone has a drink and makes introductions so that no one feels alone and everyone feels taken care of. She's become such a steady, kind presence in my classes. She has been to culinary school and has worked extensively as a private chef, and we have very similar tastes in food. I trust her to answer anything and everything, and she's become the voice for people who might have a question but feel too shy to unmute themselves. (Fun fact: Haley tested every single recipe in this book and offered invaluable feedback.)

I also love the people who attend my classes. Some of them come just once or twice, but there are also incredible regulars like Carol, who has the cutest pets; Christine, who regularly cooks along with me; and Abby, who sends me the kindest emails. Classes are multigenerational—some folks bring their kids, others their parents. Some people do it with friends and family who live in different places and then they meet on a separate Zoom after class to eat together (a long-distance couple did this for a while, which I thought was the sweetest thing). Not everyone cooks along: some people just watch and take it all in, others cook after class. Most people leave their cameras on, so it feels like we're in dozens of kitchens at the same time.

A lot of my family and close friends have also come to my classes. My parents and grandmother have been to nearly every single class. My mom takes incredibly beautiful, clever illustrated notes and my dad often cooks along, and then the three of them have an early dinner together afterward. I don't see my family in person as often as they attend classes, and whenever I see my grandma, she always says she feels like she just saw me because . . . she did. She also thinks seeing me on my mom's computer screen means I'm on a weekly television show . . . ha! Welcoming family and friends into my classes makes me feel closer to them. I like inviting them to watch me talk about this thing I love. The people in my life know I love to cook, but when they come to my classes I get to show them how I think about cooking.

I believe that teaching regularly has made me a better cook. I have a weekly opportunity to hear people's questions and answer them in real time. This allows me to deepen my thinking about the choices I make when I'm cooking and to really explain them. Teaching online has also made me a much better teacher, because people are actually in their kitchens, so I can help troubleshoot based on what tools and ingredients they have. If you have seen someone do a cooking demo in a professional kitchen with every gizmo and gadget available, it can be hard to re-create what you saw at home. When you are actually cooking in your own kitchen, though, the tips and tricks get to sink in. It's a more embodied learning experience. I also regularly mess things up, and I can embrace those moments as opportunities to think out loud and work through whatever the issue is in real time. I have burned things in class, forgotten ingredients, and more—meaning I am just a person cooking. These moments don't cause me

panic like those live demos once did. I slow down and explain my thought process in the moment, which helps me deal with whatever went wrong. Cooking, after all, is just a series of decisions.

Interacting with people in classes has also allowed me to ask everyone to share their opinions and experiences. While I'm always happy to suggest substitutions if, for example, someone is vegan or can't eat gluten, I am not actually vegan or gluten-free myself, so I'd like to know what these people think. Which flour have they had the most success with? If I get a question about how to best adjust the oven temperature for a high altitude, I check to see if anyone else in class that day lives in a similar place. It's so wonderful to have class members share their own experiences. These moments of checking in with one another have allowed me to reevaluate my feeling that being an author means having to wield some kind of authority. Teaching online reminds me over and over again how much more powerful and effective collective effort and energy are than anything I attempt alone.

I've gotten to try so many different formats and themes in my classes. I started by offering classes that were a lot like the charts in this book: "Five Salad Dressings" and "Chicken Three Ways" were two early classes. I eventually started offering classes that were complete menus: usually one or two savory dishes, plus something sweet. Before I got totally comfortable teaching, Grace suggested I have a drink just before I logged on, but then I decided to incorporate that cocktail moment into the menu (I always offer a nonalcoholic version too). Inspired by the Body Liberation Hiking Club I often join for hikes in my area of the Hudson Valley, I also started offering "No-Judgment Cooking + Eating" classes every

month, which are geared toward anyone struggling to have a loving relationship with food. We come and cook together and then, most important, we eat together while we have a conversation—often with special guests like Hannah Smith, a friend I met through the hiking group who is a therapist specializing in body image and eating disorder recovery. These classes have been very moving, and they leave us all feeling less alone and safer. I've also invited friends who are cookbook authors to join as guest teachers. And I have hosted fundraising classes for organizations that I care about, like God's Love We Deliver, Everytown for Gun Safety, the Sylvia Rivera Law Project, the National Indigenous Women's Resource Center, and World Central Kitchen. I've

done Pride classes too, and I recently started offering kids' classes, which are so much fun (kids really do ask the best questions).

I think what I love most about my classes is how relaxed and loose I feel when I'm teaching. While I take our Sunday afternoons online together seriously, the stakes feel lower than what I am doing right now—writing down something that will be printed in a book that a big company is publishing and lots of people will be selling. I love writing! And I am grateful to be a published author. But I also love that weekly chance to share my love of cooking with an extra bit of silliness. Will I teach forever? My rule for myself is that I'll stop teaching if I stop having fun or if people stop showing up. So far, neither has happened.

SECTION TWO:
VEGETABLES

STOVETOP VEGETABLES

Vegetables are my favorite thing to cook, because there are so many different kinds, they're all so interesting, you can do so many things with them, and they go with EVERYTHING. I can easily enjoy a meal without meat, fish, cheese, or eggs. But take away vegetables? I'd be lost. The way I cook them most often is a sauté-steam combination on the stovetop. I put a little fat (olive oil, butter, leftover bacon fat, etc.) in a skillet or pot and add something to flavor that fat (minced garlic, fresh ginger, dried spices, etc.), then add my vegetables (anything!), stir them around for a bit to brown them a little and coat them with the well-flavored fat, and add a little liquid to create some steam (sometimes just water, other times something that will add more flavor, such as stock, soy sauce, etc.). This gives the vegetables the benefits of both sautéing (flavor!) and steaming (tender!). I always like to finish the cooked vegetables with something bright and fresh (a squeeze of lemon, fresh herbs, a grating of salty cheese).

STOVETOP VEGETABLES	FAT & FLAVOR TO START	ADD VEG	ADD LIQUID TO STEAM THE VEG	SOMETHING FRESH TO FINISH
FAVORITE BROCCOLI RABE	OLIVE OIL, GARLIC & RED PEPPER FLAKES	BROCCOLI RABE	CHICKEN OR VEG BROTH	FRESH LEMON ZEST & JUICE
SKILLET SUCCOTASH	BUTTER & GARLIC	FROZEN LIMA BEANS, CORN & DICED ZUCCHINI	CHERRY TOMATOES & WHITE WINE	FRESH CHIVES (OR ANY HERB)
CARROTS WITH CORIANDER & CILANTRO	OLIVE OIL & GROUND CORIANDER	CARROTS	WATER & A TINY BIT OF HONEY	FRESH CILANTRO
PEPPERY ZUCCHINI WITH WHIPPED FETA	OLIVE OIL & BLACK PEPPER	ZUCCHINI	WATER	WHIPPED FETA
GINGERY BABY BOK CHOY	NEUTRAL OIL & GINGER	HALVED BABY BOK CHOY	WATER & SOY SAUCE	SCALLIONS + TOASTED SESAME SEEDS

FAVORITE BROCCOLI RABE

I'm a fan of bitter flavors like Campari and radicchio, so it's not surprising that broccoli rabe is one of my favorite vegetables. This is how I always make it, first sautéing in olive oil, garlic, and red pepper flakes, then letting it simmer with a little bit of stock, and finally finishing it with some fresh lemon zest and juice. I most often eat this as a side dish or mix it with pasta and grated cheese for a simple dinner, but another go-to is to tuck it into a sandwich with provolone and roasted peppers, just like they do at Rossi's, an Italian deli in Poughkeepsie, New York, that makes the absolute best sandwiches in the world.

Serves about 4 as a side dish

3 tablespoons olive oil

4 garlic cloves, minced

1 teaspoon red pepper flakes

1 pound broccoli rabe, tough stems discarded (trim off about 2 inches), the rest roughly chopped

½ cup chicken or vegetable broth (or boiling water mixed with Better Than Bouillon)

Kosher salt

Finely grated zest and juice of 1 lemon

Warm the olive oil in a large skillet over medium heat. Add the garlic and red pepper flakes and cook, stirring, until they begin to sizzle, about 30 seconds. Add the broccoli rabe and broth and sprinkle with a large pinch of salt. Cover and cook until the broccoli rabe has softened and is a deep green color, about 5 minutes.

Stir in the lemon zest and juice and season to taste with more salt if needed. Serve hot or at room temperature.

SKILLET SUCCOTASH

Combining corn, lima beans, zucchini, and tomatoes, succotash is one of the best ways I know to celebrate summer vegetables. You can make this any time of the year, though, with frozen corn. I love to serve it with so many things, whether it's next to eggs for breakfast, piled on toast slathered with ricotta for lunch, or as a side dish for fish, chicken, or pork for dinner. Cook it with whatever white wine you want to drink with your meal (or use dry vermouth or broth).

Serves about 4 to 6 as a side dish

3 tablespoons unsalted butter

3 garlic cloves, minced

One 12-ounce bag frozen baby lima beans (no need to defrost)

1 pound zucchini (1 large or 2 medium), diced

Kernels from 2 ears fresh corn (or 1½ cups frozen corn)

Kosher salt

1 pint cherry tomatoes, halved (see page 196 for a tip on how to halve them easily)

¼ cup dry white wine (or dry vermouth or vegetable or chicken broth)

A small handful of fresh chives, finely chopped

Place the butter and garlic in a large skillet over high heat. Once the butter melts and the garlic begins to sizzle, add the lima beans, zucchini, and corn and season them with a large pinch of salt. Cook, stirring now and then, until the vegetables begin to soften and brown in spots, about 10 minutes. Add the tomatoes and white wine and cook, stirring now and then, until most of the wine evaporates, a few minutes.

Season the succotash to taste with salt if necessary and sprinkle with the chives. Serve hot or at room temperature.

CARROTS WITH CORIANDER + CILANTRO

Coriander seeds come from cilantro plants that have gone to seed (even if you don't like cilantro, don't skip the seeds—same plant, different flavor). Combining the spice and the fresh herb is a beautiful way to pay homage to one plant. For this simple dish, you just bloom some ground coriander in olive oil, add carrots along with a little water and honey, and let them cook and get all glazed. Finished with a handful of fresh cilantro (you can substitute any other leafy herb for the cilantro, like dill or parsley), this is as good at room temperature as it is warm, making it an excellent make-ahead candidate for entertaining.

Serves about 4 as a side dish

2 tablespoons olive oil

1½ teaspoons ground coriander

1½ pounds carrots, peeled and cut into bite-sized pieces

⅓ cup water

1 tablespoon honey (or maple syrup)

½ teaspoon kosher salt

A large handful of fresh cilantro (mostly leaves, but some tender stems are fine!), roughly chopped

Place the olive oil in a large skillet over medium heat. Add the coriander and cook, stirring, until it begins to sizzle, about 30 seconds. Add the carrots, water, honey, and salt and bring the mixture to a boil, then lower the heat to a simmer and cook, uncovered, until the carrots are slightly softened and most of the water has evaporated, about 10 minutes. Season to taste with more salt if needed.

Serve hot or at room temperature, sprinkled with the cilantro.

PEPPERY ZUCCHINI WITH WHIPPED FETA

There are a lot of things I love about this recipe. One is that it treats black pepper as the magnificent spice that it is, rather than just a little something to sprinkle on top of a dish. Its spiciness really comes through when you toast it in olive oil. Another thing I love is that you don't have to be afraid to really brown the zucchini to develop its sweetness, something we often miss when we just cook it quickly without allowing it to develop color and flavor. The final thing I love is the whipped feta, which is just feta whizzed in the food processor and thinned with a little buttermilk. It is smooth and rich and just the most amazing bed for the peppery zucchini. Try whipped feta with other vegetables, such as roasted squash or a platter of ripe tomato slices.

Serves about 4 as a side dish

3 tablespoons olive oil

1 teaspoon freshly ground black pepper, plus more for the feta

1 pound zucchini (about 2 medium), cut into bite-sized pieces

Kosher salt

¼ cup water

¼ pound feta cheese

2 tablespoons buttermilk (or regular whole milk)

Place the olive oil in a large skillet over medium-high heat. Add the pepper and cook, stirring, until it begins to sizzle, about 30 seconds. Add the zucchini with a large pinch of salt and cook, stirring, until it begins to brown in spots, about 5 minutes. Add the water, bring to a boil, and cook, uncovered, until the zucchini is slightly softened and most of the water has evaporated, about 4 minutes. Season to taste with more salt if needed.

Meanwhile, place the feta and buttermilk in the bowl of a food processor and blitz, scraping down the sides with a rubber spatula as needed, until smooth, creamy, and whipped. Season to taste with salt and pepper.

Spread the whipped feta on your serving platter and top with the zucchini. Serve warm or at room temperature.

GINGERY BABY BOK CHOY

When I worked at Long Season Farm (see page 107), one of the tasks I did most often was harvest bok choy. I would cut each head from the ground with a paring knife, and I took great pleasure in picking the best-looking bok choy from each row. When cooking with it, I much prefer the smallest heads, aka baby bok choy. I cut each one lengthwise in half through the stem, put the halves in a big bowl of cold water, and swish them around so any dirt falls to the bottom of the bowl. Then I lift them out and let them hang out on a kitchen towel while I sizzle the ginger in some oil. I add the bok choy and let it brown, then steam it with water and soy sauce. It's so good!

Serves about 4 as a side dish

3 tablespoons neutral oil (such as vegetable, grapeseed, or canola)

One 2-inch piece fresh ginger, peeled and cut into matchsticks

1 pound baby bok choy, split lengthwise in half

¼ cup water

2 tablespoons soy sauce

3 scallions, ends trimmed, thinly sliced

1 teaspoon toasted sesame seeds (if yours aren't already toasted, toast them in the dry skillet first, set them aside, and proceed with the recipe)

Place the oil in a large skillet over high heat. Add the ginger and cook, stirring, until it begins to sizzle, about 30 seconds. Add the bok choy, split side down, and cook, without turning it, until the undersides are browned, about 5 minutes. Drizzle the water and soy sauce, cover the skillet, and cook until the bok choy is tender, about 2 minutes.

Transfer the bok choy to a serving platter and sprinkle with the scallions and sesame seeds. Serve warm or at room temperature.

ROASTED VEGETABLES

Making delicious roasted vegetables is so simple: just coat your vegetables with olive oil and salt, spread them out on a sheet pan (don't pack them too tightly), and roast at 425°F until browned and tender. You can add other things like chickpeas or nuts to the vegetables, if you'd like. Once everything is cooked, finish with something acidic and interesting just to balance the sweet roasted flavors. This could be as quick as a lemon squeezed over the vegetables, or as complex as homemade salsa macha (page 90) or carrot-miso dressing (page 88). I think this final step is the most crucial, and it brings so much dimension to the otherwise plain sheet pan of veggies.

ROASTED VEGETABLES	COAT WITH OLIVE OIL, SALT & ROAST	FINISH WITH SOMETHING ACIDIC AND INTERESTING
ROASTED SQUASH AGRODOLCE	DELICATA SQUASH	VINEGAR, HONEY & GARLIC
ROASTED BRUSSELS SPROUTS WITH SHERRY VINAIGRETTE + MANCHEGO	BRUSSELS SPROUTS	SHERRY VINAIGRETTE & MANCHEGO
ROASTED BROCCOLI w/ CARROT-MISO DRESSING	BROCCOLI	CARROT-MISO DRESSING
ROASTED SWEET POTATOES WITH SALSA MACHA	SWEET POTATOES	SALSA MACHA
ROASTED GREEN BEANS WITH WALNUTS & LEMON	GREEN BEANS & WALNUTS	LEMON

ROASTED SQUASH AGRODOLCE

Delicata squash is my favorite variety of winter squash because it doesn't have to be peeled, its thin skin is easy to cut through, and it tastes great (win, win, win). Roasting it for a little while to start and then tossing it with a mixture of vinegar, honey, and garlic and cooking it for a bit longer yields a slightly sour-and-sweet ("agrodolce") dish. It's just as wonderful served warm as it is at room temperature, making it a great make-ahead option. Feel free to top the squash with roasted nuts, herbs, something creamy (crème fraîche, labneh . . . whatever!), or dried fruit (golden raisins would be great) . . . or just serve as is!

Serves about 4 as a side dish

2 delicata squash

2 tablespoons extra-virgin olive oil

Kosher salt

1 tablespoon sherry vinegar (or red wine vinegar)

2 tablespoons honey (or maple syrup)

1 garlic clove, minced

Preheat your oven to 425°F.

Thinly slice off and discard the ends of the squash. Cut each squash lengthwise in half. Use a spoon to scrape out and discard the seeds, then cut each squash crosswise into half-moon pieces that are about ¼ inch thick. Place the squash on a sheet pan, drizzle with the olive oil, sprinkle with a large pinch of salt, toss everything together, and spread the squash out in an even layer. Roast, stirring occasionally, until the squash is just tender and beginning to brown, about 20 minutes.

While the squash is roasting, whisk together the vinegar, honey, and garlic in a small bowl.

Drizzle the vinegar mixture over the almost-done squash and toss well to combine. Continue to roast until the squash is a little bit glazed and a bit more browned, about 5 minutes. Transfer to a serving platter and serve hot or at room temperature.

ROASTED BRUSSELS SPROUTS
WITH SHERRY VINAIGRETTE + MANCHEGO

Like a little trip to Spain, these crispy sprouts are doused with a sherry vinegar dressing and showered with Manchego cheese. To add a bit more texture and highlight another excellent Spanish ingredient, you could also top them with some chopped Marcona almonds. Serve these alongside almost anything, including, but not limited to, roast chicken, grilled steak, or pan-seared fish.

Serves about 4 as a side dish

For the sprouts:

1½ pounds Brussels sprouts, trimmed and halved

3 tablespoons olive oil

Kosher salt and freshly ground black pepper

For the vinaigrette:

1 garlic clove, minced

1½ tablespoons sherry vinegar

1 teaspoon honey (or maple syrup)

3 tablespoons extra-virgin olive oil

Kosher salt and freshly ground black pepper to taste

To finish:

2 ounces Manchego cheese, thinly shaved with a vegetable peeler (about ½ cup)

First, roast the sprouts: Preheat your oven to 425°F.

Place the sprouts on a sheet pan. Drizzle with the olive oil, sprinkle with about ½ teaspoon salt, grind over lots of black pepper, and use your hands to mix everything together. Spread the sprouts out in an even layer. Roast, stirring once or twice, until they are softened and browned in spots, about 25 minutes.

Next, make the vinaigrette: Place all the vinaigrette ingredients together in a serving bowl, whisk well to combine, and taste for seasoning.

Finish the dish: When the sprouts are done, add them to the bowl with the vinaigrette and mix well to combine. Top with the Manchego and serve hot or at room temperature.

ROASTED BROCCOLI WITH CARROT-MISO DRESSING

Okay, I have a few things I want to tell you here. First, the broccoli gets so sweet and a little crunchy when you roast it, and the carrot-miso dressing would make anything taste good, even a shoe. Next, if you have an air fryer, feel free to use it for the broccoli. Toss it with the oil and salt and air-fry at 400°F for 15 minutes, shaking the basket halfway through. Lastly, this makes a full cup of dressing, so you'll likely have some left over. Keep it in your fridge and use it for a simple romaine or iceberg salad, or for a platter of tomatoes, or as a dip for almost anything, including . . . carrots!

Serves about 4 as a side dish

For the broccoli:
2 pounds broccoli, tough stems discarded, cut into large florets

¼ cup olive oil

Kosher salt

For the dressing:
1 medium carrot, peeled and roughly chopped

1 tablespoon minced fresh ginger

1 tablespoon white miso paste

1 tablespoon honey (or maple syrup)

3 tablespoons unseasoned rice vinegar

2 tablespoons water

1 tablespoon toasted sesame oil

¼ cup olive oil

½ teaspoon kosher salt

½ teaspoon freshly ground black pepper (or white pepper, if you have it)

Roast the broccoli: Preheat your oven to 425°F.

Place the broccoli on a sheet pan, drizzle with the olive oil, and sprinkle with a big pinch of salt. Toss everything well to combine, then spread the broccoli out in an even layer. Roast the broccoli, stirring it now and then, until softened, browned, and crisp on the edges, about 20 minutes.

Meanwhile, make the dressing: Place everything in the pitcher of a blender and puree until supersmooth. That's it!

To serve, place the broccoli on a serving platter and drizzle with the dressing, or serve the dressing in a small bowl alongside for dipping.

ROASTED SWEET POTATOES WITH SALSA MACHA

Salsa macha is a wonderful mix of fried chiles, garlic, peanuts, and sesame seeds all seasoned with a tiny bit of sugar, some salt, and some vinegar. It's complex and layered, and it is a great complement to roasted sweet potatoes. If you have any leftovers, try the salsa on your eggs in the morning, or use it on grilled fish for delicious fish tacos. Dried chiles can be found at Mexican markets and often in the produce section of other grocery stores.

Serves about 4 to 6 as a side dish

For the sweet potatoes:

2 pounds sweet potatoes, scrubbed, cut into bite-sized pieces

2 tablespoons olive oil

Kosher salt

For the salsa macha:

½ cup neutral oil (such as vegetable, grapeseed, or canola)

2 dried ancho chiles, stems and seeds removed

2 dried chiles de árbol, stems and seeds removed

2 garlic cloves, thinly sliced

¼ cup salted roasted peanuts, roughly chopped

2 teaspoons white sesame seeds (toasted or untoasted, either is fine)

2 teaspoons white vinegar (or any other type of vinegar)

1 teaspoon light or dark brown sugar

½ teaspoon kosher salt

Roast the sweet potatoes: Preheat your oven to 425°F.

Place the sweet potatoes on a sheet pan, drizzle with the olive oil, and sprinkle with a big pinch of salt. Toss well to combine and spread the potatoes out in an even layer. Roast the sweet potatoes, stirring them now and then, until softened, browned, and crisp on the edges, about 45 minutes.

Meanwhile, make the salsa macha: Place the oil in a small heavy saucepan over medium-high heat. Add one dried chile to the oil, and when it begins to sizzle, add the rest of the chiles, garlic, peanuts, and sesame seeds. Cook, stirring frequently, until the chiles are puffed and the garlic is light brown, about 3 minutes. Carefully transfer the mixture to a small heatproof serving bowl and let cool to room temperature.

Stir the vinegar, brown sugar, and salt into the chile mixture. Transfer to the bowl of a food processor and pulse until the chiles and peanuts are finely chopped and the salsa is the texture of a coarse pesto. Season to taste with more vinegar, sugar, and/or salt if needed. Transfer the salsa macha back to the serving bowl.

To serve, place the sweet potatoes on a serving platter with the bowl of salsa macha for everyone to spoon on top of their potatoes as they wish.

ROASTED GREEN BEANS WITH WALNUTS + LEMON

This side dish is all about the simplicity of roasting everything together on one sheet pan: green beans, thinly sliced lemon, and walnuts. They all get browned and a little sweet. Feel free to substitute any nut you like for the walnuts (if you have already roasted nuts, skip the roasting step and just top the roasted green beans with them). Serve with virtually anything, from the simplest meal of store-bought rotisserie chicken to a big holiday spread.

Serves about 4 as a side dish

1 pound green beans, topped and tailed

1 lemon, thinly sliced

½ cup raw walnuts, roughly chopped

3 tablespoons extra-virgin olive oil

½ teaspoon kosher salt

Preheat your oven to 425°F.

Place the green beans, sliced lemon, and walnuts on a sheet pan. Drizzle with the olive oil, sprinkle with the salt, and use your hands to mix everything together, then spread out in an even layer.

Roast, stirring once or twice, until the green beans and lemon slices are softened and browned in spots and the walnuts are wonderfully toasted, about 25 minutes.

Serve the beans warm or at room temperature.

STUFFED VEGETABLES

Filling vegetables—anything from peppers to squash—with a flavorful stuffing before cooking them is a beautiful way to give them the grandeur they deserve. Stuffed vegetables make for excellent side dishes, but they can also be the stunning centerpiece of a meal. To make great ones, fill the vegetables with a stuffing made of something starchy (cooked rice, breadcrumbs, etc.) for bulk, something fatty (bacon, feta, butter, etc.) for flavor and moisture, and, of course, something flavorful to season it all (spices, garlic, lemon zest, etc.). Once you join the stuffed vegetable party, it's hard to go back—they're just so much fun.

STUFFED VEGETABLES	VEGETABLE WITH A CAVITY	SOMETHING STARCHY FOR THE FILLING	SOMETHING FATTY	FLAVOR!
FETA + RICE-STUFFED PEPPERS	BELL PEPPERS	COOKED RICE & FROZEN SPINACH	FETA	GARLIC POWDER & DRIED OREGANO
TWICE-BAKED CACIO E PEPE POTATOES	BAKED POTATOES (SCOOPED OUT)	FLUFFY POTATO FROM ←	PECORINO & BUTTER	TONS OF BLACK PEPPER
MUSHROOMS ROCKEFELLER	MUSHROOMS WITH STEMS POPPED OFF	CHOPPED MUSHROOM STEMS, BREADCRUMBS & SPINACH	BUTTER & PARMESAN	GARLIC, LEMON ZEST & JUICE
TOMATOES CASINO	TOMATOES (SCOOPED OUT)	BREADCRUMBS	BACON!	GARLIC & FRESH PARSLEY
SPICED CHICKPEA SQUASH BOWLS	ROASTED ACORN SQUASH (HALVED & SEEDED)	CHICKPEAS + CRUSHED TOMATOES	OLIVE OIL	LOTS OF SPICES & CILANTRO

FETA + RICE-STUFFED PEPPERS

A lovely option for vegetarian guests, these peppers feel extra special because each one comes with its own little hat. I use half a 10-ounce bag of frozen spinach for this recipe. You can also use 5 ounces of fresh spinach (the size of most baby spinach containers at the grocery store): just wilt it in a pot or sauté it before adding it to the stuffing mixture. These are especially great to make if you have leftover cooked rice in your fridge (if not, cook ⅓ cup rice, and you'll be good to go). Like all stuffed vegetables, these can be assembled ahead of time and baked just before serving.

Makes 4 peppers

4 large bell peppers (any color you want)

2 tablespoons olive oil

Kosher salt

1 cup cooked rice (white or brown, or any grain really!)

¼ pound feta cheese, crumbled

5 ounces frozen chopped spinach (no need to defrost unless it's in a block)

1 tablespoon garlic powder

2 teaspoons dried oregano

1 cup chicken or vegetable broth (or boiling water mixed with Better Than Bouillon)

Preheat your oven to 375°F.

Cut the tops off the peppers (reserve them) and use a small spoon to scoop out and discard the seeds and ribs from each one, being careful to keep the peppers intact.

Stand the peppers in a baking dish and drizzle the cavities with the olive oil. Season the interior of each pepper with a large pinch of salt.

Place the rice, feta, spinach, garlic powder, and oregano in a large bowl and mix well to combine. Season the mixture to taste with salt. Divide the filling evenly among the cavities of the peppers, place the tops on the peppers, and pour the broth around them (not over them!). Roast until the filling is hot and the peppers are a bit softened, about 1 hour.

Serve hot or at room temperature.

TWICE-BAKED CACIO E PEPE POTATOES

Filled with grated pecorino, butter, and black pepper, these potatoes have all the flavor of cacio e pepe pasta with the cozy satisfaction of a baked potato (there's also a little sour cream because it helps keep the filling from drying out). You can bake your potatoes up to a few days in advance, then make the filling and bake them for the second time just before serving. Or prepare them all the way through, cool, and refrigerate, then warm them back up in a 300°F oven until piping hot, about 20 minutes, before serving.

Makes 8 potato halves

4 large baking potatoes

4 tablespoons (½ stick) unsalted butter, melted

½ cup sour cream

¾ cup finely grated pecorino cheese

1 teaspoon kosher salt

1 teaspoon freshly ground black pepper

Preheat your oven to 425°F.

Pierce each potato in a few places with a fork or a paring knife (this will help the steam escape as they cook). Place the potatoes directly on the middle oven rack and bake until they are easily pierced with a paring knife or a thin skewer, about 1 hour.

Transfer the potatoes to a cutting board (leave the oven on). Carefully cut each potato lengthwise in half. Once they're cool enough to handle, scoop out nearly all the flesh from each potato half, leaving enough in each one to create a sturdy shell (like a canoe), and transfer the flesh to a large bowl.

Add the butter, sour cream, ½ cup of the pecorino, and the salt and pepper to the warm potato flesh and use a fork or potato masher to crush everything together well, then give the mixture a few stirs with a large spoon to make sure all the ingredients are thoroughly combined. Divide the mixture evenly among the potato shells (it's okay if they seem overstuffed; that makes them fun).

Line a sheet pan with foil or parchment, place the potatoes on it, and sprinkle the tops with the remaining ¼ cup cheese. Return the potatoes to the oven and bake until the tops are golden brown and crisp, about 20 minutes. Serve hot.

MUSHROOMS ROCKEFELLER

Absolutely one of my all-time favorite appetizers, this dish takes the flavors of oysters Rockefeller (garlic, spinach, cheese, lemon) and puts them in mushroom caps. If you're making them for vegan friends, use olive oil or nondairy butter instead of the regular butter and substitute a tablespoon of nutritional yeast for the cheese. If you end up with leftover filling (it depends on the size of your mushroom caps), try stirring it into cooked pasta or adding it to your next batch of meatballs.

Makes 2 dozen stuffed mushrooms

2 dozen cremini or button mushrooms (about 1½ pounds), wiped clean

4 tablespoons (½ stick) unsalted butter

4 garlic cloves, minced

One 10-ounce package frozen chopped spinach, defrosted, squeezed dry

Kosher salt

½ cup panko breadcrumbs

½ cup finely grated Parmesan cheese

Finely grated zest and juice of 1 lemon

Preheat your oven to 425°F.

Pop the stems off the mushrooms and finely chop the stems (you can do this by hand or in the bowl of a food processor).

Place the butter and garlic in a large skillet over medium heat. Once the butter melts and the garlic begins to sizzle, add the mushroom stems and spinach and season with a large pinch of salt. Cook, stirring now and then, until most of the moisture has evaporated, about 6 minutes. Turn off the heat and stir in the panko, Parmesan, lemon zest, and lemon juice. Season the mixture to taste with salt.

Use a small spoon to distribute the spinach mixture evenly among the mushrooms, placing it in the cavities the now-gone stems left behind. Line up the mushrooms, stuffed side up, on a sheet pan.

Roast the mushrooms until they are softened and the tops are lightly browned, about 15 minutes. Let the mushrooms cool for a few minutes, then serve hot.

TOMATOES CASINO

Oh gosh, I love these. Making them is one of my favorite ways to use up a bunch of ripe tomatoes. With all the flavors of clams casino (bacon, garlic, parsley), they are a great appetizer on their own, and wonderful served on soft polenta or spaghetti to make a more complete meal. Once I happened to make them on the same day I made Frozen-Fish Chowder (page 125) and then stuck one of the tomatoes into each bowl of soup, and the result was unbelievable. Feel free to add goat cheese or blue cheese to the filling if you'd like to make these extra rich.

Makes 6 tomatoes

6 vine-ripened tomatoes

¼ cup olive oil, plus a little bit for the baking dish

¼ pound bacon, diced

4 garlic cloves, minced

1 cup panko breadcrumbs

A small handful of fresh flat-leaf parsley, finely chopped

Kosher salt

Preheat your oven to 425°F.

Use a serrated knife to cut a thin slice off the top and bottom of each tomato and then use a spoon to scoop out the centers of each one (discard the stem and reserve the pulp). When scooping, you don't have to hollow out the entire thing—you want to keep each tomato intact; you're basically looking to create tomato cups. Finely chop the tomato pulp and reserve it.

Place the olive oil and bacon in a skillet over medium heat and cook until the bacon is browned and crisp around the edges, about 5 minutes. Add the garlic and cook just until it sizzles, about 30 seconds. Turn off the heat and stir in the tomato trimmings, panko, and parsley. Season the mixture to taste with salt.

Place a little oil in the bottom of a baking dish (about a tablespoon at most) and use your fingertips to coat the dish with the oil. Put the tomatoes hollowed side up in the dish. Season the interior of each tomato with a large pinch of salt and then divide the panko mixture among the tomatoes.

Roast the tomatoes until they have browned a bit and are nice and soft but have not given up their shape entirely, about 25 minutes.

Serve hot or warm.

SPICED CHICKPEA SQUASH BOWLS

These are a perfect fall or winter vegetarian entrée. I love making them with acorn squash because their cavities are so large, but you can also use delicata squash (cut in half lengthwise and scoop out the seeds), or make "mini" squash bowls with honeynut squash halves. These happen to be totally vegan and are great drizzled with a simple tahini sauce (like the one in the Rice + Lentil Bowl with All the Toppings on page 183), or you can try topping them with some crumbled feta cheese (so no longer vegan, but delicious). If you don't like cilantro, just skip it!

Makes 4 stuffed squash halves

2 acorn squash, halved through the stems, seeds scooped out and discarded

About 7 tablespoons olive oil

Kosher salt

1 small yellow onion, finely diced

2 garlic cloves, minced

1 teaspoon ground cumin

1 teaspoon ground coriander

½ teaspoon ground cinnamon

½ teaspoon sweet pimentón (smoked Spanish paprika)

One 15-ounce can chickpeas, drained and rinsed

One 15-ounce can crushed tomatoes

A large handful of fresh cilantro (mostly leaves, but some tender stems are fine), chopped

Preheat your oven to 400°F.

Place the squash cavity side up on a sheet pan. Drizzle each squash with about a tablespoon of oil and then use your fingers to coat the squash with the oil. Season each squash half generously with salt.

Roast the squash until it's just tender when pierced with a paring knife, 30 to 45 minutes, depending on the squash.

While the squash is roasting, place the remaining 3 tablespoons oil in a skillet over medium heat and add the onion, garlic, spices, and a large pinch of salt. Cook, stirring now and then, until the onion is softened, about 10 minutes. Add the chickpeas and tomatoes and turn the heat to high. Once the mixture comes to a boil, turn down the heat and let it simmer for 15 minutes to combine and deepen the flavors. Turn off the heat, stir in the cilantro, and season the chickpeas to taste with salt.

Divide the chickpeas among the squash halves and serve hot or at room temperature.

THAT TIME I WAS A FARMER

After writing *Simply Julia*, I thought I was done with cookbooks. Between my own books and the collaborative work I've done with other authors, it was the fifteenth book I had worked on in as many years. I was burned-out.

But one day in January 2021, a couple of months before *Simply Julia* came out, I was picking up our CSA share from Long Season Farm, the best vegetable farm in our area. Bill, one of the LSF farmers, asked me how I was doing. I answered him truthfully: "Burned-out," I told him.

"You know," he said, "we need someone for next season's crew." His comment planted a seed.

I had been friendly with Bill and his bosses, Sam and Erin, who own and run the farm, for a while. I'd first met them years ago as a customer at the farmers market, and then in 2020, I basically invited myself to be a sort of intern. It was a few months after lockdown, and I was itching to be around other people in a safe way. Helping out at the farm offered that, plus it was a great place to channel some of my anxiety about the pandemic. There are so many things to do on a vegetable farm, and participating in those physical tasks outdoors allowed me to feel a little calmer and more connected to my community.

I got home that January day with our CSA share and told Grace I thought maybe I would apply for a job at the farm. I said it might be a way for me to step away from making cookbooks but still stay close to food. I could be outside all day working with my hands and not have to be the decision-maker. I could be part of a team without being in charge of anything. And I could work on distancing myself from social media simply by leaving my phone in the car while I was at the farm all day. Grace supported my decision to go for it.

Sam and Erin sent me their official job description. For the first time in my long freelance, word-of-mouth career, I wrote a résumé and formally applied for a job. When I submitted everything, I included this note:

I will be honest, my résumé doesn't bode very well for farming experience, but it definitely speaks to my long love of food and my long appreciation for farming. You two know firsthand the extent of my farming experience, which is to say it's not much, but I believe myself to be a fast and eager learner, and I am grateful to possess a positive attitude, physical strength, and stamina.

I believe spending a season being part of the Long Season Farm crew would allow me to continue developing my knowledge of food, but in a completely different way than I have previously pursued. I am excited at the prospect of doing work that actively engages my body, gives me a way to spend more time outside, and, most importantly, allows me to be part of a team. I am skilled at working independently, but also long for the camaraderie of a team that's led with clear direction and expectations.

I know bringing me on might require some more instruction/time on your part and appreciate your consideration.

A few months later, I found myself in new work boots and a big straw hat reporting to work at the farm. I have two pictures of myself from my first day. The first is a selfie I took in my car before I drove home. I look so happy and content. The second is a picture of my left hand covered with a thin layer of dirt, evidence of my hard day at work. When I look back at these photos now, I remember the excitement of trying something new and jumping right into the deep end.

I spent seven months working on the Long Season crew, and I learned so much in that time. A lot of what I learned was practical, like how to use a sharp hoe to agitate dirt *just so* to loosen weeds, and that it's best to give each section of a seedling tray a little squeeze before popping out the plants. I learned that my years of loving to buy, cook, and eat vegetables had given me great intuition about harvesting vegetables. I know, for example, just by feel, when a bunch of kale is the right size. I know when a cauliflower is big enough to cut from its cozy leaves and how many radishes to bundle with a rubber band.

But the biggest takeaways were more personal. I learned how liberating it was to immerse myself in a new challenge. It's a joy to realize everyone has something to teach if you're up for asking questions. I learned that I can really talk all day (farming is incredibly social!). You spend so much time working with other people doing repetitive tasks like making bunches of greens, tying up tomato and pepper plants with twine to help them stand up tall, and digging carrots from the ground. Tasks like these occupy your body and require attention, but not so much attention that you can't have a little conversation. I learned that I like these types of conversations, ones that come and go as one person moves farther down the row than the other, conversations that can be picked back up anytime. I learned that I like to drive a big van and an old pickup truck. I learned that even if it feels scary, I can speak up when I think things could run more smoothly. I learned that I love working outside and really enjoy working with other people who also do. I learned that I love lifting heavy things. I learned that I can tolerate really hot days, especially if I acclimate to them by starting off early in the morning when it's cool and just lean into it. "You will be hot, but you will be okay," I'd silently remind myself. I learned that I can handle cold and wind and working in the rain and even kind of get a kick out of it. I learned that I am tougher than I thought.

As I write this, it's been two years since I stopped working full-time at LSF, but I still go there all the time. I pick up whatever produce didn't sell at the market every week and take it to our local food pantry, and I usually help the crew one morning every week or so in the season. I go back because I like the work and I like the people. I like that it reminds me that cookbooks may still be part of my life but the world of cookbooks doesn't have to consume my whole life. I like remembering how much work goes into producing the ingredients that I so love to cook. I like reminding myself that there are people behind everything we eat and that, for a time, I was one of them.

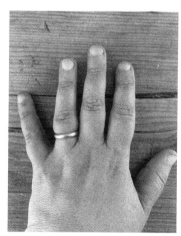

SECTION THREE:
SOUPS, STEWS & BRAISES

BROTHY SOUPS

Gosh, I love making soup. It lets me clear out the fridge and extend the little bits of this and that hanging around. It's usually a one-pot situation. Leftover soup only gets better after a couple of days in the fridge, and freezes well. It's there for us. It's easygoing. Some people might say, "But soup isn't a full meal!" To them I say, eat more than one bowl! Also, add garlic bread.

To make brothy soups, I recommend cutting up some vegetables (it could just be one onion, could be a lot of things) and sautéing them in a little olive oil in your soup pot until they're soft. Add seasonings, if you want (spices, garlic, etc.), and then add the liquid (water, broth, canned tomatoes, a little cream, whatever you like) and things that can simmer until soft—greens, pasta, beans, meatballs, etc. Toppings are a fun way to introduce more flavor and texture, a little freshness, too, maybe even some heat: herbs, grated cheese, a squeeze of lemon or lime, croutons, hot sauce. You get the idea! Eat the soup out of a bowl or put it in a mug. Enjoy it while working on a puzzle. Give yourself permission to go to bed at 8:30 p.m. That is soup life, and I am into it.

BROTHY SOUPS	SAUTÉ IN OLIVE OIL	ADD LIQUID	ADD THIS & SIMMER	TOP WITH
FASTEST CHICKEN NOODLE SOUP	DICED CHICKEN BREASTS + CARROTS WITH GARLIC POWDER & PAPRIKA	CHICKEN BROTH	EGG NOODLES/ RAW GARLIC AT THE VERY END	FRESH HERBS (OPTIONAL)
ITALIAN WEDDING SOUP	ONIONS & GARLIC	CHICKEN BROTH	SMALL MEATBALLS, SMALL PASTA & GREENS	GRATED PECORINO
MINESTRONE-ISH	ONION, CARROTS, CABBAGE, GARLIC, TOMATO PASTE + DRIED OREGANO	CANNED TOMATOES + CHICKEN OR VEG BROTH	CANNED WHITE BEANS & SMALL PASTA	GRATED PARM & STORE-BOUGHT PESTO
ANY-BEAN SOUP	DICED ONION, CARROTS + LOTS OF GARLIC	CHICKEN OR VEG BROTH	DRIED BEANS	LOTS OF FRESH HERBS & OLIVE OIL DRIZZLE
FROZEN-FISH CHOWDER	DICED ONION & CELERY	SEAFOOD OR FISH BROTH & CREAM	DICED POTATOES, CORN & FISH	FRESH CHIVES & OYSTER CRACKERS

FASTEST CHICKEN NOODLE SOUP

This is truly the quickest chicken noodle soup ever: once you've cut up your chicken and carrots, it takes about 15 minutes. Seriously! And it's just about the most comforting pot of food I know. After cooking the chicken and carrots with some seasoning, you just add boiling water and Better Than Bouillon paste (see page 160 for my love letter to this stuff) and egg noodles. Once those are cooked, stir in some minced raw garlic (crucial), and then serve topped with herbs, if you'd like. Note that the longer this soup sits on low heat, the more the noodles will soften and absorb the broth. This is not a bad thing! Just a thing to be aware of if you don't think you and yours will consume all the soup, or most of it, in one sitting. And leftovers can always be stretched with extra broth.

Makes about 3 quarts (serves about 6 to 8)

¼ cup olive oil

1½ pounds boneless, skinless chicken breasts, cut into bite-sized pieces

2 large (or 3 medium) carrots, peeled, cut into bite-sized pieces

2 teaspoons kosher salt

2 teaspoons garlic powder

2 teaspoons sweet paprika

10 cups boiling water (or not boiling, but the soup will take a little longer to cook)

2 tablespoons Better Than Bouillon Roasted Chicken Base

One 12-ounce package wide egg noodles

2 large garlic cloves, minced

For serving: Chopped fresh dill and/or flat-leaf parsley (optional)

Place the oil in a large heavy pot (such as a Dutch oven) over high heat. Add the chicken and carrots and season with the salt, garlic powder, and paprika. Cook, stirring now and then, until the chicken is opaque all over and just firm, about 8 minutes (it's okay if it's not totally cooked through at this point).

Add the water to the pot and whisk in the Better Than Bouillon. Bring the pot to a boil (this should be nearly instant if you're using boiling water) and then turn the heat down to medium. Stir in the egg noodles and cook, stirring every so often, until they're just tender, about 6 minutes.

Stir the minced garlic into the soup, season to taste with more salt if needed, and serve, with herbs sprinkled on top, if desired.

ITALIAN WEDDING SOUP

No ceremony is required for this cozy soup (the name "wedding soup" is actually said to come from the idea of the greens, meatballs, and broth coming together in a harmonious way . . . like a wedding!). The meatballs are cooked directly in the soup, which makes them very tender and makes for a one-pot meal as well, but if you'd like, you can roast them first so they're a bit firmer. Just put them on a parchment-lined sheet pan in a 400°F oven until they're browned, about 25 minutes, then add them to the soup. It's an extra step and extra cleanup, but it's a nice option and I want you to have all the options!

Makes about 4 quarts (serves about 8)

For the meatballs:

1 small yellow onion

1 large egg

2 teaspoons dried oregano

2 teaspoons garlic powder

1 teaspoon kosher salt

1 pound lean ground beef (or ground turkey)

½ cup breadcrumbs (I use panko, but you can use whatever you have—and feel free to use gluten free crumbs)

For the soup:

¼ cup extra-virgin olive oil

1 large yellow onion, chopped

Kosher salt

6 garlic cloves, minced

8 cups chicken broth (or boiling water mixed with Better Than Bouillon)

1 small head escarole, leaves separated, cleaned, coarsely chopped (or a 12-ounce package frozen spinach)

1 cup small pasta (ditalini, orzo, orecchiette, elbows—whatever you have! Regular or gluten-free!)

For serving: Grated pecorino cheese and freshly ground black pepper

Make the meatballs: Using the largest holes on a box grater, coarsely grate the onion into a medium bowl. It will be very liquidy, and that is okay! Add the egg and seasonings and mix well to combine. Use your hands to mix in the meat, then mix in the breadcrumbs. Form the meat mixture into small meatballs (you're aiming for about 2 dozen), placing them on a plate as you work. Set them aside while you get the soup going.

Make the soup: Place the oil in a large heavy pot (such as a Dutch oven) over medium heat. Add the chopped onion and a large pinch of salt and cook, stirring now and then, until the onion just begins to soften, about 5 minutes. Add the garlic and cook, stirring, until very fragrant, about a minute.

Add the chicken broth, turn the heat to high, and bring the mixture to a boil. Season to taste with salt. Turn the heat down to a simmer. Gently add the meatballs to the pot and simmer, uncovered, for 10 minutes, just to get them started cooking. As they cook, a little froth will float to the top—you can use a large spoon to lift this off and discard it (don't stress about it, though; it's okay if you don't get it all).

Add the escarole and pasta to the pot, stirring them in very gently (you don't want to break up the meatballs). Simmer the soup, stirring gently every now and then, until the greens are softened and the pasta is just tender, about 10 minutes.

Serve the soup hot with lots of grated pecorino and black pepper on top.

MINESTRONE-ISH

This falls somewhere on the soup spectrum between minestrone and pasta fagioli; it's full of vegetables, with deep tomato flavor from lots of tomato paste, and hearty from a mix of beans and pasta. Topped with grated cheese and a dollop of pesto, it's a satisfying vegetarian soup. But if you want to make it extra special, try Haley's Savory Sprinkles, which are the most delicious lemony breadcrumbs (see below for the recipe).

Makes about 3 quarts (serves about 6 to 8)

¼ cup extra-virgin olive oil

1 yellow onion, chopped

4 carrots, peeled and chopped

Kosher salt

6 garlic cloves, minced

3 tablespoons tomato paste

1 teaspoon dried oregano

1 pound green cabbage, roughly chopped (about 8 cups chopped cabbage)

One 15-ounce can beans (I recommend cannellini, chickpeas, or small red beans), drained and rinsed

One 28-ounce can diced tomatoes

6 cups chicken or vegetable broth (or boiling water mixed with Better Than Bouillon)

1 cup small pasta (ditalini, orzo, orecchiette, elbows—whatever you have! Regular or gluten-free!)

For serving: Grated Parmesan cheese, freshly ground black pepper, and pesto (homemade or store-bought), and/or Haley's Savory Sprinkles (recipe follows)

Place the oil in a large heavy pot (such as a Dutch oven) over medium heat. Add the onion, carrots, and a large pinch of salt and cook, stirring now and then, until the vegetables are beginning to soften, about 5 minutes. Add the garlic, tomato paste, and dried oregano and cook, stirring, until very fragrant, about a minute.

Add the cabbage, beans, diced tomatoes with their juice, and the broth, turn the heat to high, and bring the mixture to a boil. Season to taste with salt. Reduce the heat to low and simmer, uncovered, until the cabbage is softened and the flavors are very well combined, at least 30 minutes (but it's fine for up to an hour or two over very low heat, if that helps to know). Just before you're ready to eat, add the pasta and cook until softened, about 10 minutes or so.

Serve the soup hot with lots of grated cheese, freshly ground black pepper, a spoonful of pesto, and/or a shower of Haley's Savory Sprinkles in each bowl.

HALEY'S SAVORY SPRINKLES

Place 2 tablespoons olive oil in a skillet over medium-high heat. Add a cup of coarse fresh breadcrumbs (or panko) and cook, stirring, until golden brown, about 5 minutes. Remove from the heat and let the breadcrumbs cool for a couple of minutes, then stir in the finely grated zest of a lemon and ½ cup of grated Parmesan (or ¼ cup nutritional yeast, if vegan). Season to taste with salt and pepper.

ANY-BEAN SOUP

This incredibly simple recipe is really just a formula for well-seasoned beans cooked in plenty of liquid so you get beans and a delicious bean broth all in one pot. Bean cooking times depend on the type and age of the beans you're cooking, so if yours take a while (hands-off time!) and so much of the liquid in the pot evaporates that the beans are exposed, just add a splash more broth as you're cooking. No biggie.

You can use dried lentils instead of beans, if you'd like. You can also use a can or two of beans or lentils (just drain and rinse them first), reduce the broth to 3 or 4 cups, and reduce the simmering time to just 20 minutes to meld all the flavors. If you want to make this soup thicker, you can blend a little bit of it and return it to the pot (or blend it all for a smooth soup!). Lastly, you can add a few handfuls of finely chopped kale or cabbage (or any other vegetables you'd like) toward the end of cooking. So many options!

Makes about 2 quarts (serves about 4)

¼ cup extra-virgin olive oil

1 yellow onion, chopped

4 carrots, chopped

Kosher salt

6 garlic cloves, minced

1 cup dried beans (any type you'd like, just know that the cooking time varies)

6 cups chicken or vegetable broth (or boiling water mixed with Better Than Bouillon), plus more if needed

For serving: Chopped fresh flat-leaf parsley or any herb you'd like (or no herbs! Or pesto!) and olive oil

Place the oil in a large heavy pot (such as a Dutch oven) over medium heat. Add the onion, carrots, and a large pinch of salt and cook, stirring now and then, until the vegetables are beginning to soften, about 5 minutes. Add the garlic and cook, stirring, until very fragrant, about a minute.

Add the beans and broth to the pot, turn the heat to high, and bring the mixture to a boil. Season to taste with salt. Reduce the heat to low and simmer, uncovered, until the beans are softened, anywhere from 1 to several hours, depending on the type of bean. If the mixture gets too thick before the beans are softened, just add more broth (you might need anywhere from another cup to a full quart, depending on the bean cooking time and how brothy you like the soup).

Season the soup to taste with salt and serve hot, with a sprinkling of herbs and a drizzle of oil on each serving.

A BIT MORE ABOUT BEANS!

Type of Bean (or Legume)	Approx. Cooking Time	Additional Notes
GARBANZO (A.K.A. CHICKPEAS)	~1 HOUR	THE MOST VERSATILE?!
PINTO BEANS	~1-2 HOURS	SOOO COMFORTING!
BLACK BEANS	~1-2 HOURS	BFFS WITH CUMIN & OREGANO
CANNELLINI	~2 HOURS	A BLANK SLATE
FRENCH LENTILS	~1/2 HOUR	HOLD THEIR SHAPE
RED LENTILS	~20 MINS.	GET VERY SOFT

MORE INFO

DRY CUP AMOUNT	DRY WEIGHT	COOKED AMOUNT	CAN AMOUNT
1/2 CUP	.2 POUND	~1 1/2 CUPS	1 CAN
1 CUP	.4 POUND	~3 CUPS	2 CANS
2 CUPS	.8 POUND	~6 CUPS	3 CANS
2 1/2 CUPS	1 POUND	~7 CUPS	4 CANS

FROZEN-FISH CHOWDER

I just love this recipe. It's so FAST (under 30 minutes) and convenient, especially because any type of frozen fish works and you don't even need to defrost it before cooking.

Makes about 2½ quarts (serves about 6)

¼ cup extra-virgin olive oil

1 yellow onion, chopped

4 large celery stalks, finely diced

1 teaspoon Old Bay Seasoning (optional)

Kosher salt

4 cups seafood or fish broth (or chicken or vegetable, or boiling water mixed with Better Than Bouillon)

1 cup heavy cream

1 pound frozen cod fillets (or any firm white fish; no need to defrost)

1 large Russet potato, peeled and diced

One 16-ounce package frozen corn kernels (no need to defrost; or kernels from 4 ears fresh corn)

Freshly ground black pepper

For serving: Minced fresh chives and oyster crackers

Place the oil in a large heavy pot (such as a Dutch oven) over medium heat. Add the onion, celery, Old Bay, if using, and a large pinch of salt and cook, stirring now and then, until the vegetables are beginning to soften, about 5 minutes.

Add the broth and cream. Turn the heat to high and bring the mixture just to a boil. Season to taste with salt if needed. Add the fish, potatoes, and corn and bring the the mixture to a boil. Immediately turn the heat down to low and simmer, uncovered, until the fish is cooked through and the potatoes are tender, about 15 minutes. As you stir the soup, the fish should break up into pieces. If it doesn't, just simmer a little longer so it flakes more easily, and then give it all a good stir.

Season the chowder to taste with salt and pepper. Serve hot, with minced chives and oyster crackers scattered over each bowl.

PUREED SOUPS

Sautéing or roasting vegetables for pureed soups gives you the opportunity to build lots of flavor in that initial cooking before liquid enters the picture. I find a ratio of 2 pounds of vegetables to 4 to 6 cups of liquid to be about right. But remember, it's soup. It's flexible. It's casual.

A few things to keep in mind:

- When adding the liquid, start with less than you think you might need and then add more as necessary (way easier to add than having to take some of it away).

- When using a regular blender, puree the soup in batches and be careful not to fill the blender more than halfway. Start blending on low before gradually increasing the speed, and be sure to vent the steam through the opening in the lid (I like to put a kitchen towel on top of the hole to prevent splatters!).

- You can also use an an immersion blender, which, in my opinion, is one of the most underrated—and affordable—kitchen appliances out there. With an immersion blender there's no need to work in batches, as you can puree directly in your pot, and there's barely anything to clean up. I also love using an immersion blender to puree just a portion of the soup, creating a texture that is full-bodied but not totally smooth.

- Have fun with toppings! Especially with pureed soups, adding some contrasting texture and/or flavors makes things more interesting.

PUREED SOUPS ≡	SAUTÉ OR ROAST VEGETABLES (~2 POUNDS)	ADD LIQUID (4-6 CUPS)	PUREE & TOP WITH SOMETHING GOOD
ROASTED SQUASH SOUP	WHOLE ROASTED SQUASH & SAUTÉED ONIONS WITH GARLIC & CORIANDER	VEG. BROTH & COCONUT MILK	SOUR CREAM & TOASTED PUMPKIN SEEDS
CARROT GINGER SOUP	CARROTS, ONION, & A TON OF GINGER	SAME AS ↗	STORE-BOUGHT RED CHILE OIL (OR CHILE CRISP)
RED CURRY CORN SOUP	ONIONS, FROZEN CORN, A DICED POTATO & RED CURRY PASTE	SAME AS ↗	CORN NUTS
CREAMY TOMATO & COCONUT SOUP	ONION & GARLIC	CANNED TOMATOES & COCONUT MILK	TOASTED UNSWEETENED COCONUT FLAKES
SPICY SWEET POTATO SOUP	WHOLE ROASTED SWEET POTA-TOES/SAUTÉED ONIONS + GARLIC	VEG. BROTH	SOUR CREAM & HOT SAUCE

ROASTED SQUASH SOUP

I love butternut squash but hate the peeling and seeding it requires. For this soup, you get to skip all that work and just prick the squash with a fork and roast it whole (as if it were a baked potato); then, after you let it cool, the skin and seeds are so, so, so much easier to remove. You can do this any time you want pureed squash. For this soup, you just combine the roasted squash with sautéed onions and garlic and blend with coconut milk and a little vegetable broth. It's creamy and rich, and it happens to be totally vegan (minus the sour cream topping). A great Thanksgiving starter!

Makes nearly 2 quarts (serves about 4 to 6)

1 large butternut squash
(about 2½ to 3 pounds)

¼ cup extra-virgin olive oil

1 large yellow onion, chopped

4 garlic cloves, minced

1 teaspoon ground coriander

Kosher salt

One 13.5-ounce can full-fat
coconut milk (or 1½ cups
half-and-half)

1 cup vegetable broth
(or boiling water mixed with
Better Than Bouillon),
plus more if needed, depending
on how big your squash is

For serving: Sour cream and
toasted pumpkin seeds

Preheat your oven to 400°F.

Pierce the squash in a few places with a fork or a paring knife. Place it on a foil-lined sheet pan and roast, turning occasionally, until very soft (test with a paring knife), about an hour. Remove from the oven, carefully cut the squash in half to let steam escape, and let it cool until you can handle it.

Meanwhile, place the oil in a large heavy pot (such as a Dutch oven) over medium heat. Add the onion, garlic, coriander, and a large pinch of salt and cook, stirring now and then, until the onion just begins to soften, about 5 minutes. Add the coconut milk and vegetable broth and turn the heat to high. Once the mixture just comes to a boil, reduce the heat to low and simmer while you tend to your squash. Season the soup to taste with salt as needed.

When the squash is cool enough to handle, remove the seeds and skin. Add the squash to the soup and use an immersion blender to puree everything together (or do this in batches in the pitcher of a regular blender). If the soup is too thick, add a bit more broth. Season to taste with salt.

Serve the soup hot, topped with sour cream and toasted pumpkin seeds.

CARROT GINGER SOUP

Packed with flavor from both fresh and dried ginger, this soup is incredibly comforting. I like to finish it with a swirl of chile oil (or chile crisp), but a spoonful of sour cream or crème fraîche would also be very welcome. Sometimes I serve the soup with grilled cheese sandwiches for a fun spin on the classic tomato soup combo (which I also love; I just like to shake things up every now and again) for a very cozy and satisfying meal.

Makes nearly 2 quarts (serves about 4 to 6)

¼ cup extra-virgin olive oil

2 pounds carrots, peeled and roughly chopped

1 large yellow onion, chopped

One 3-inch piece fresh ginger, peeled and finely chopped

2 teaspoons ground dried ginger

Kosher salt

One 13.5-ounce can full-fat coconut milk (or 1½ cups half-and-half)

3 cups vegetable broth (or boiling water mixed with Better Than Bouillon)

For serving: Store-bought chile oil (or chile crisp)

Place the oil in a large heavy pot (such as a Dutch oven) over medium heat. Add the carrots, onion, and fresh and dried ginger and season with a large pinch of salt. Cook, stirring now and then, until the vegetables begin to soften, about 10 minutes.

Add the coconut milk and vegetable broth and turn the heat to high. Once the mixture just comes to a boil, lower the heat to a simmer and season to taste with salt (the exact amount depends on how salty your broth is). Cover the pot and cook until the carrots are incredibly tender, about 20 minutes.

Use an immersion blender to puree everything together (or do this in batches in the pitcher of a regular blender). Season the soup to taste with salt and serve hot, topped with chile oil.

RED CURRY CORN SOUP

Like the Vegetable + Tofu Coconut Curry (page 142), this soup gets much of its flavor from store-bought curry paste. (I regularly use Mae Ploy, which includes shrimp paste, or Mama Lam's if I want to make a vegan version; you can order either from umamicart.com or find curry paste in your local Asian market.) I love serving this topped with crunchy corn nuts to echo the corn flavor in the soup, but you could also try thinly sliced scallions or chopped fresh cilantro. If you'd like a less smooth soup, you can skip the pureeing and end up with a wonderful twist on an old-fashioned corn and potato chowder!

Makes nearly 2 quarts (serves about 4 to 6)

¼ cup extra-virgin olive oil

1 large yellow onion, chopped

1 large Russet potato, peeled and diced

One 10-ounce package frozen corn kernels (no need to defrost)

Kosher salt

2 tablespoons Thai or Malaysian red curry paste (see headnote)

One 13.5-ounce can full-fat coconut milk (or 1½ cups half-and-half)

3 cups vegetable broth (or boiling water mixed with Better Than Bouillon)

For serving: Corn nuts (optional)

Place the oil in a large heavy pot (such as a Dutch oven) over medium heat. Add the onion, potato, and corn, season with a large pinch of salt, and cook, stirring now and then, until the vegetables just begin to soften, about 10 minutes.

Stir in the curry paste, coconut milk, and vegetable broth and turn the heat to high. Once the mixture just comes to a boil, lower the heat to a simmer and season to taste with salt (the exact amount depends on how salty your broth is). Cover the pot and cook until the potatoes are incredibly tender, about 15 minutes.

Use an immersion blender to puree everything together (or do this in batches in the pitcher of a regular blender). Season the soup to taste with salt and serve hot topped with corn nuts, if using.

CREAMY TOMATO + COCONUT SOUP

Tomatoes and coconut are such good friends, and I love combining them in this creamy soup. Since it's made with a can of tomatoes and a can of coconut milk, it comes together very quickly. If you want a heftier soup, chickpeas would be a wonderful addition (you can add them before or after blending, depending on whether you want the soup to be totally smooth or smooth with pops of chickpeas). Serve this with sandwiches or a hearty salad for a complete meal, or serve as a starter course for a longer meal (I suggest following it up with Spicy Chicken with Lime + Cashews, page 228, lots of hot rice, and Gingery Baby Bok Choy, page 81).

Makes nearly 2 quarts (serves about 4 to 6)

¼ cup coconut oil

1 large yellow onion, chopped

4 garlic cloves, minced

Kosher salt

One 28-ounce can whole peeled tomatoes

One 13.5-ounce can full-fat coconut milk

1 cup vegetable broth (or boiling water mixed with Better Than Bouillon)

1 tablespoon fresh lime juice (or sherry vinegar)

For serving: Toasted unsweetened coconut flakes

Place the oil in a large heavy pot (such as a Dutch oven) over medium heat. Add the onion and garlic, season with a large pinch of salt, and cook, stirring now and then, until the onion just begins to soften, about 5 minutes.

Add the tomatoes with their juice, coconut milk, and vegetable broth and turn the heat to high. Once the mixture just comes to a boil, lower the heat to a simmer and season to taste with salt (the exact amount depends on how salty your broth is). Cover the pot and cook for just a bit to really meld all the flavors, about 10 minutes.

Use an immersion blender to puree everything together (or do this in batches in the pitcher of a regular blender). Stir in the lime juice and season the soup to taste with salt. Serve hot, topped with coconut flakes.

SPICY SWEET POTATO SOUP

Anytime I'm baking sweet potatoes, I make a few extra and use the leftovers for this sweet-and-spicy soup. If you're cooking for someone who doesn't like heat, you can skip the cayenne; or, if you'd like an extra-hot soup, feel free to add a minced fresh jalapeño in addition to the cayenne. This is a great fall soup, and I would serve it with just about any type of sandwich.

Makes nearly 2 quarts (serves about 4 to 6)

2 pounds sweet potatoes (about 3 large potatoes)

¼ cup extra-virgin olive oil

1 large yellow onion, chopped

6 garlic cloves, minced

1 to 3 teaspoons cayenne pepper (1 for mild, 2 for medium, 3 for hot)

Kosher salt

4 cups vegetable broth (or boiling water mixed with Better Than Bouillon)

For serving: Sour cream and hot sauce

Preheat your oven to 375°F.

Pierce each sweet potato in a few places with a fork or a paring knife. Place them on a foil-lined sheet pan and roast, turning occasionally, until very soft (test with a paring knife), about an hour. Remove from the oven, carefully cut the sweet potatoes in half to let steam escape, and let them cool until you can handle them.

Meanwhile, place the oil in a large heavy pot (such as a Dutch oven) over medium heat. Add the onion, garlic, cayenne, and a large pinch of salt and cook, stirring now and then, until the onion just begins to soften, about 5 minutes. Add the broth and turn the heat to high. Once the mixture just comes to a boil, lower the heat to a simmer and season to taste with salt (the exact amount depends on how salty your broth is).

When the sweet potatoes are cool enough to handle, remove and discard the skin. Add the sweet potatoes to the soup and use an immersion blender to puree everything together (or do this in batches in the pitcher of a regular blender).

Season the soup to taste with salt. Serve hot, topped with sour cream and hot sauce.

STEWS

Soups, stews, and braises all have similar foundations, and I'd say the major difference between the three is the amount of liquid: soup is made with things submerged in liquid, stews are made with things nearly covered in liquid, and braises include just enough liquid to get everything tender as it cooks.

To make a great stew, you want to first sauté the base ingredients, then add enough liquid to nearly cover them and simmer until everything is fall-apart-y. I like to serve stews on or with a delicious carbohydrate (rice, polenta, tortilla chips, etc.) to sop up all the flavorful cooking juices and top with something to add a little extra brightness and texture (pickled chiles, herbs, hot sauce, cheese . . . you get it!).

STEWS	SAUTÉED BASE	ADD ALL OF THIS & SIMMER	SERVE ON/WITH	TOPPINGS!
MUSHROOM CACCIATORE	OLIVE OIL, MUSHROOMS, ONION, PEPPERS & LOTS OF FLAVORFUL SEASONINGS	RED WINE, CANNED TOMATOES & OLIVES	PASTA or POLENTA	GRATED CHEESE
JENNIE'S CURRIED CHICKEN & POTATOES	CHICKEN SEASONED WITH JAMAICAN CURRY POWDER, GARLIC POWDER & ONION POWDER	WATER, POTATOES & CARROTS	WHITE RICE	HOT SAUCE
VEGETABLE & TOFU COCONUT CURRY	ONION & CURRY PASTE IN COCONUT OIL	VEGETABLES & TOFU	RICE or NOODLES	PEANUTS, CILANTRO, SCALLIONS, FRIED ONIONS, HOT SAUCE... ANYTHING!
TURKEY & GREEN CHILE CHILI	OLIVE OIL, GROUND TURKEY, ONION, GARLIC & SPICES	CANNED GREEN CHILES, TOMATOES & BEANS	RICE, CORNBREAD, TORTILLA CHIPS, OR WARM TORTILLAS	HOT SAUCE, SOUR CREAM, CILANTRO, AVOCADO, PICKLED JALAPEÑOS... ANYTHING!
TOMATO, WHITE BEAN & FENNEL STEW	OLIVE OIL, GARLIC & SLICED FENNEL	CANNED WHITE BEANS, TOMATOES & VEG BROTH	PASTA, RICE, POLENTA OR GARLIC BREAD	FENNEL FRONDS

MUSHROOM CACCIATORE

The secret ingredient here is porcini powder, which is simply ground dried porcini mushrooms; it adds an incredible depth of flavor. You can get it from thespicehouse.com or from Kalustyan's online store. You can also use a coffee grinder to grind dried porcini to a fine powder. Or you can simply leave it out! The cacciatore will still be excellent. If you do get the powder, use the leftovers to season steak or any meat before grilling or add it to mushroom soup, mushroom risotto, mushroom . . . anything.

Serves about 4 generously

¼ cup olive oil, plus more if needed

1 pound cremini mushrooms, cleaned (leave them whole; the stems are fine here!)

1 large yellow onion, finely chopped

1 red bell pepper, cored and seeded, diced

6 garlic cloves, minced

1 tablespoon minced fresh rosemary

1 tablespoon porcini powder

2 tablespoons tomato paste

2 teaspoons kosher salt

2 teaspoons dried oregano

½ cup red wine (or vegetable broth with a splash of red wine vinegar)

One 28-ounce can whole peeled tomatoes

1 cup pitted olives (black, green, whatever you want . . . my favorites are Castelvetrano)

For serving: Cooked pasta or polenta and lots of grated Parmesan or pecorino cheese

Place the oil in a large heavy pot (such as a Dutch oven) over medium-high heat. Add the mushrooms and cook, stirring now and then, until they are browned all over and look glossy, about 5 minutes. Transfer the mushrooms to a bowl.

If your pot is dry, add a splash of oil. Add the onion and bell pepper and cook, stirring now and then, until they just begin to soften, about 5 minutes. Add the garlic, rosemary, porcini powder, tomato paste, salt, and oregano and cook, stirring, just until super fragrant, about 30 seconds.

Add the wine, turn the heat to high, and bring the mixture to a boil; while this is happening, use a wooden spoon to scrape up any stuck-on bits at the bottom of the pot. Let the wine mixture boil for a minute, then add the tomatoes, olives, and reserved mushrooms. Once the mixture comes back up to a boil, turn the heat to low and cover, with the lid slightly ajar to let some steam escape. Cook, stirring now and then and breaking up the tomatoes a bit as you stir, until all the flavors have melded, about 20 minutes. Season to taste with salt.

Serve the cacciatore hot over pasta or polenta, with plenty of grated cheese on top.

If you're familiar with any of my previous cookbooks, you know that Jennie is one of the most important people in my life. She was my babysitter for a decade, starting when I was three years old, and we continue to be very close. Jennie's cooking is the food that always makes me feel most at home. Her curried chicken is like a hug. To make it, seek out Jamaican curry powder (try your local Caribbean market, if you have one, or ask if you can buy some from your neighborhood Caribbean restaurant; or find it online). Neither Jennie nor I favor one brand more than another, but Blue Mountain Country is widely available and very good!

Serves about 4 generously (more like 6 people if you serve it with lots of rice)

1 whole chicken, cut into parts (you can ask a butcher to do this or do it yourself), or 6 bone-in, skin-on chicken thighs

2 teaspoons kosher salt

2 tablespoons Jamaican curry powder

1 tablespoon garlic powder

1 tablespoon onion powder

2 tablespoons neutral oil (such as vegetable, grapeseed, or canola)

1 yellow onion, thinly sliced

2 cups water

1 pound Yukon Gold potatoes, peeled and cut into bite-sized pieces

1 pound carrots, peeled and cut into bite-sized pieces

For serving: Cooked white rice and hot sauce

Place the chicken pieces in a large bowl and sprinkle with the salt and curry powder, garlic powder, and onion powder. Use your hands to rub all the seasonings into the chicken. Cover the bowl and let the chicken sit at room temperature for an hour, or marinate in the refrigerator for up to 24 hours (take it out of the refrigerator 1 hour before cooking).

Place the oil in a large heavy pot (such as a Dutch oven) over medium-high heat and brown the seasoned chicken all over, about 10 minutes total (do this in batches if necessary). Stir together the browned chicken and the onion, then pour in the water, turn the heat to high, and bring the mixture to a boil. Turn the heat to low, cover the pot, with the lid slightly ajar to let some steam escape, and cook until the chicken is completely cooked through and on its way to very tender, about 45 minutes.

Stir the potatoes and carrots into the stew. If they're not covered with liquid, add a little more water to the pot so that they're *just* submerged (you're not making soup, so they don't have to be swimming—just enough liquid so that the vegetables get nice and soft). Cover the pot and cook until the chicken and vegetables are all very tender, about another 45 minutes.

Season the stew to taste with salt and serve hot over white rice with hot sauce on the side for anyone who would like some.

VEGETABLE + TOFU COCONUT CURRY

I make this incredibly quick, versatile meal all the time. My favorite curry paste brand is Mae Ploy (I like their Massaman curry paste best). It lasts for a long time in the refrigerator and does all the work of building flavor for you. Note that many curry pastes contain shrimp, and if that's an issue for you, seek out a vegan one, like Mama Lam's.

You can use any vegetables for this curry (great options include potatoes, carrots, cabbage, cauliflower, spinach, peas, zucchini, bell peppers, and snap peas). If you're using a mix of firm, hard vegetables (like potatoes and carrots) and quick-cooking vegetables (like spinach), add the harder vegetables first and cook until nearly tender, then add the quicker-cooking vegetables. Serve this with rice, noodles, or roasted sweet potatoes you've split open . . . or just a bowl and a spoon! Add any toppings you'd like, including but not limited to: chopped toasted peanuts, chopped cilantro, thinly sliced scallions, store-bought fried onions, toasted coconut flakes, minced fresh chile peppers, and/or hot sauce.

Makes about 2 to 3 quarts (serves about 4 to 6)

2 tablespoons coconut oil

1 yellow onion, diced

Kosher salt

3 tablespoons Thai or Malaysian curry paste (any flavor you like)

One 13.5-ounce can full-fat coconut milk

1 to 2 pounds mixed vegetables (fresh or frozen!), cut into bite-sized pieces as necessary

One 14-ounce package firm tofu, drained, cut into bite-sized pieces

For serving: Cooked rice, roasted sweet potatoes, or noodles and toppings of your choice (all optional)

Place the coconut oil in a medium pot over medium heat, add the onion and a big pinch of salt, and cook, stirring now and then, until the onion begins to soften, about 5 minutes. Stir in the curry paste and let it fry a little bit to wake up all the flavors, about a minute. Whisk in the coconut milk. Fill the coconut milk can halfway with water, swish it around, and add the water to the pot. Turn the heat to high, and when the mixture just begins to boil, turn it down to medium-low. Season the mixture to taste with salt.

Add the longest-to-cook vegetables (potatoes, carrots, etc.), cover the pot, and simmer until they are just tender (the exact time depends on what vegetables you're using, but figure about 10 to 15 minutes for dense stuff like root vegetables). Then, once those are tender, add the tofu and any faster-to-cook vegetables, including frozen vegetables. (If all your vegetables are about the same density, you can just add everything at once.) Simmer until all the vegetables are tender, about 5 to 10 more minutes or so.

Serve hot over rice, sweet potatoes, or noodles (or just in a bowl). Top with whatever you'd like to top it with!

I have made countless pots of chili and written numerous recipes for different types of chili. This is the one I keep coming back to, because it has so much flavor from the generous amounts of cumin, pimentón, and canned green chile peppers. Plus, it's so simple to prepare. To make this vegan, just substitute an extra can of beans for the ground turkey. Serve with your favorite toppings (I've given you a few ideas below). To turn this pot of food into a more substantial meal, serve with cornbread, tortilla chips, warm corn or flour tortillas, quesadillas, or rice.

Makes nearly 2 quarts (serves about 4)

¼ cup olive oil

1 pound ground turkey (preferably not super lean—the more fat, the better!)

Kosher salt

1 large yellow onion, finely diced

6 garlic cloves, minced

1 tablespoon ground cumin

2 teaspoons sweet pimentón (smoked Spanish paprika)

One 7-ounce can (or two 4-ounce cans) roasted green chile peppers (with their juice)

One 28-ounce can diced tomatoes

One 15-ounce can beans (I suggest using pinto, cannellini, navy, or black beans), NOT drained

For serving: Toppings of your choice, such as hot sauce, sour cream, grated cheddar cheese, sliced avocado, cilantro, pickled jalapeños, and/or sliced scallions

Place the oil in a large heavy pot (such as a Dutch oven) over medium-high heat. Use your hands to break the turkey into small pieces as you add it to the pot. Season generously with salt and cook, stirring now and then, until it's a little bit browned, about 10 minutes.

Add the onion, garlic, cumin, pimentón, and a big pinch of salt and cook, stirring now and then, until the onion begins to soften and brown in spots, about 10 minutes.

Add the chile peppers with their liquid, the tomatoes with their juice, the beans with their liquid, and another big pinch of salt. Bring the mixture to a boil, then immediately lower the heat to a gentle simmer. Cover with the lid slightly ajar, to let some steam escape, and cook, stirring now and then, until all the flavors have melded, about 20 minutes.

Season the chili to taste with salt one final time and serve with the toppings of your choice.

TOMATO, WHITE BEAN + FENNEL STEW

A simple combination of fresh fennel, canned beans, and canned tomatoes, this stew can be turned into a complete meal by serving with pasta, rice, polenta, or garlic bread. It can also be the base for a simple fish or shellfish meal. Just put a few white fish fillets or a pound of shrimp, clams, or mussels on top of the stew when it has just about finished cooking, cover, and simmer until cooked through. Lovely!

Makes about 1½ quarts (serves about 4)

1 large head fennel, any browned outer layers removed

¼ cup olive oil

6 garlic cloves, minced

1 teaspoon fennel seeds

One 15-ounce can white beans, drained and rinsed

One 28-ounce can whole peeled tomatoes

½ cup vegetable broth (or boiling water mixed with Better Than Bouillon)

Kosher salt

For serving: Cooked pasta, rice, or polenta or garlic bread

If your fennel has the fronds and long stalks attached, cut them off, roughly chop the fronds, and reserve them for garnish. Thinly slice the long stalks (as if each were a celery stalk) and thinly slice the fennel bulb. Reserve.

Place the oil in a large heavy pot (such as a Dutch oven) over medium-high heat. Add the garlic and fennel seeds and cook, stirring, just until super fragrant, about 30 seconds. Add the sliced fennel stems and bulb and stir to coat with the garlicky oil.

Add the beans, tomatoes, vegetable broth, and a large pinch of salt. Turn the heat to high and bring the mixture to a boil. Immediately turn the heat to low, cover with the lid slightly ajar, to let some steam escape, and cook, stirring now and then, until the fennel has softened and all the flavors have melded, about 20 minutes. Season to taste with salt.

Serve hot over pasta, rice, polenta, or garlic bread, with the reserved chopped fennel fronds sprinkled on top.

BRAISES

Braising is such a gorgeous way to coax flavors out of whatever you're cooking. To braise something means to first brown the ingredients in a skillet or pot with just a little fat, then add only enough liquid to come up the sides of whatever you're cooking (don't submerge!), turn the heat down, and simmer until your food is tender and infused with flavor. You can braise just about anything from tofu (quick!) to a pork shoulder (a few hours to transform it from tough into something meltingly soft). The ingredients you brown, the liquid, and the seasonings are so fun to play around with. For example, the Braised Pork with Apricots + Green Olives could easily be made with chicken thighs or chuck roast instead of pork. The cooking liquid could be apple cider, wine, or even just water instead of chicken broth. And the apricots and green olives could be replaced by prunes and capers. The possibilities are endless.

BRAISES	BROWN THIS	ADD THIS LIQUID	ADD THIS & SIMMER	TOP/SERVE WITH
BRAISED EGGPLANT W/ TOMATOES + GOLDEN RAISINS	PIECES OF EGGPLANT	CRUSHED TOMATOES	GOLDEN RAISINS & CAPERS	FOCACCIA OR CRUSTY BREAD
SOY-BRAISED TOFU WITH SCALLIONS	SCALLIONS, GARLIC + GINGER	WATER, SOY SAUCE + HONEY	TOFU	RICE
BRAISED FISH WITH CREAM & DILL	ONIONS	WHITE WINE & CREAM	FISH	FRESH DILL
CHICKEN SCARPARI-ELLO	SAUSAGE + FLOURED CHICKEN, PLUS ONIONS, PEPPERS & GARLIC	WHITE WINE & CHICKEN BROTH	RETURN THE SAUSAGE & CHICKEN TO THE POT	PASTA!
BRAISED PORK WITH APRICOTS + GREEN OLIVES	PORK SHOULDER	CHICKEN BROTH	DRIED APRICOTS & GREEN OLIVES	BUTTERED EGG NOODLES OR CREAMY POLENTA

BRAISED EGGPLANT WITH TOMATOES + GOLDEN RAISINS

Okay, I never want anyone, including me, to use two pots or pans when you can get away with one, but in this instance, both a nonstick skillet and a pot are required. The nonstick skillet makes browning the eggplant much easier; not only does it not stick, but you also don't need to use a bucket of oil to keep it from sticking (olive oil is not cheap!). Finishing the braised eggplant in a larger pot then ensures that you won't have tomato sauce splattered everywhere and you'll have room to really stir everything together. I love this eggplant hot or at room temperature served with plenty of focaccia or any crusty bread to mop up the sauce. It's also great as part of a spread of Italian food, like a platter of sliced fresh mozzarella, maybe some melon and prosciutto, a simple arugula salad . . . you get the idea! You can also serve it as a vegan entrée on top of polenta.

Makes about 2 quarts (serves about 6 as an appetizer or about 4 as a main dish)

½ cup olive oil

1 large heavy eggplant, ends trimmed, cut lengthwise in half and then into 2-inch pieces

One 28-ounce can crushed tomatoes

2 garlic cloves, minced

2 teaspoons kosher salt

½ cup golden raisins

2 tablespoons drained capers

For serving: Focaccia or your favorite crusty bread, toasted if you'd like

Place half the oil in a large nonstick skillet over medium-high heat. Add half the eggplant pieces and cook, turning the pieces as they color, until deeply browned all over, about 10 minutes. Transfer the browned eggplant to a large heavy pot (such as a Dutch oven) and reserve it in the pot while you repeat the browning process with the remaining oil and eggplant in your skillet.

Once all the eggplant is cooked and is waiting in the pot, add the tomatoes, garlic, salt, raisins, and capers to it and stir everything well to combine. Set the pot over medium-high heat, bring it to a boil, then turn the heat down to low, cover the pot with the lid slightly ajar, to let some steam escape, and cook, stirring now and then, until the eggplant has softened and all the flavors have melded, about 1 hour. Season to taste with salt.

Serve hot, warm, or at room temperature, with lots of focaccia or crusty bread.

SOY-BRAISED TOFU WITH SCALLIONS

This recipe is so quick and easy, and it's one of my favorite ways to enjoy tofu. By cutting scallions into big pieces and browning them quickly, you're really able to capture their sweetness. I think they're the star of this show as much as the tofu! Note that the tofu in this recipe is soft (which I personally love), but if you prefer that it have a crispier exterior, feel free to first brown it in the skillet before continuing with the recipe (or coat the cubes with about 2 tablespoons of cornstarch, spray with cooking spray, and cook for 15 minutes in a 400°F air fryer).

Serves about 2 to 4, depending on appetites and side dishes

2 tablespoons neutral oil (such as vegetable, grapeseed, or canola)

2 bunches scallions, ends trimmed, cut into 1-inch pieces

Kosher salt

6 garlic cloves, minced

One 2-inch piece fresh ginger, peeled and minced

3 tablespoons water

2 tablespoons soy sauce

1 tablespoon honey (or maple syrup)

One 14-ounce block firm tofu, drained, patted dry with a towel, cut into 1-inch cubes

For serving: Cooked rice

Place the oil in a large nonstick skillet over medium-high heat. Add the scallions, season with a large pinch of salt, and cook, stirring now and then, until slightly softened and browned in spots, about 3 minutes.

Add the garlic and ginger and cook just until fragrant, about 30 seconds. Add the water, soy sauce, and honey and turn the heat to high. Stir well as the mixture comes to a boil, then lower the heat to medium-low. Add the tofu and cook, stirring gently now and then, until the sauce thickens slightly and the tofu is piping hot, about 5 minutes.

Serve hot with rice.

SOUPS, STEWS & BRAISES 153

BRAISED FISH WITH CREAM + DILL

Most braised dishes call for browning the protein, adding some vegetables and liquid, and then simmering away. This simple, quick braise starts with browning the vegetables (onions) and then adding the fish and liquid. This means you get the flavor from the browned onions and you don't have to worry about your fish sticking to the pot, plus it will cook gently (making this a great method to try for anyone nervous about cooking fish). If using frozen fish, either defrost it first or cook from frozen and add about 10 minutes to the cooking time. Serve with rice or mashed potatoes.

Serves about 4

2 tablespoons olive oil

1 large yellow onion, thinly sliced

Kosher salt

½ cup dry white wine (or dry vermouth, or vegetable or chicken broth)

1 cup heavy cream

1 pound fresh or frozen cod fillets (or any other firm white fish)

A large handful of fresh dill, finely chopped

Place the oil in a large heavy pot (such as a Dutch oven) over medium-high heat. Add the onion and season with a large pinch of salt. Cook, stirring now and then, until the onion begins to soften and brown in spots, about 5 minutes. Add the white wine, turn the heat to high, and let the mixture boil for a full minute to cook off some of the alcohol and to develop flavor.

Add the cream. Once the mixture comes back to a boil, immediately lower the heat so it simmers gently. Season to taste with salt and then add the fish to the pot.

Cover and simmer until the fish is cooked through (it should flake easily when you poke it with a fork), about 15 minutes. Uncover the pot, sprinkle the dill on top of everything, and serve immediately.

CHICKEN SCARPARIELLO

Chicken scarpariello, which means "shoemaker's chicken," has always been one of my favorite things to order at Italian-American restaurants. It's also a great make-ahead dish, as it tastes even better the next day (after the chicken cools down, you can shred it into the cooking juices, if you'd like). Serve with spaghetti dressed simply with garlic, olive oil, and Parmesan (or with red sauce), plus a chopped romaine salad with Pizzeria Vinaigrette (page 24). If you can't find sliced cherry peppers, just slice whole ones (be sure to save the brine from the jar to mix into the chicken).

Serves about 4

¼ cup olive oil, plus more if needed

1 pound fresh sweet or hot Italian sausage links (pork, turkey, or chicken)

2 bone-in, skin-on chicken breasts, cut crosswise in half with a good heavy knife (you can have your butcher do this, too, or leave them whole, or use 4 bone-in, skin-on chicken thighs)

Kosher salt and freshly ground black pepper

A small handful of flour (all-purpose or gluten-free) for dusting

1 yellow onion, thinly sliced

1 red bell pepper, cored and seeded, thinly sliced

One 10-ounce jar sliced cherry peppers (spicy or mild—up to you!)

4 garlic cloves, minced

1 teaspoon dried oregano

½ cup dry white wine (or dry vermouth or additional chicken broth)

1 cup chicken broth (or boiling water mixed with Better Than Bouillon)

Place the oil in a large heavy pot (such as a Dutch oven) over medium heat. Add the sausage links and cook, turning them now and then, until thoroughly browned all over, about 8 minutes. Transfer the sausage links to a plate.

While the sausage is browning, season the chicken pieces generously with salt and pepper and dust with a little flour.

Once the sausage is out of the pot, add the chicken and cook, turning once, until browned on both sides, about 4 minutes per side. Transfer the chicken to the plate with the sausage.

There should still be some fat in the bottom of the pot; if not, add a glug of oil. Add the onion and bell pepper to the fat and season with a big pinch of salt. Cook, stirring now and then to scrape up any browned bits stuck to the bottom of the pot, until the vegetables just begin to soften, about 5 minutes. Add the cherry peppers (including their brine), garlic, oregano, and white wine, bring the mixture to a boil, and let it boil for a minute to cook off some of the alcohol. Add the chicken broth to the pot.

Cut the browned sausage links into 1-inch pieces and return them to the pot, along with the chicken plus whatever juices have accumulated on the plate. Lower the heat so that the mixture simmers, cover the pot, and cook until the chicken is very tender, about 45 minutes.

Season the braising liquid to taste with more salt and pepper and serve.

BRAISED PORK WITH APRICOTS + GREEN OLIVES

Sweet apricots and salty olives create a rich backdrop for tender pork in this dish. If you'd prefer to do the slow cooking in your oven rather than on the stovetop, tuck the covered pot into a 300°F oven for a few hours. If you want the meat to be very shredded, let it cool completely and then use your hands instead of forks or tongs (it's nice to wear a pair of disposable gloves).

Serves about 6

One 3-pound boneless pork shoulder roast (or pork butt or Boston butt), trimmed of any large pieces of fat or gristle, cut into 4 even pieces

2 teaspoons kosher salt

2 tablespoons olive oil

1½ cups chicken broth (or boiling water mixed with Better Than Bouillon)

4 dried bay leaves

1 cup dried apricots

1 cup pitted green olives, preferably Castelvetrano

2 large sprigs fresh rosemary

For serving: Buttered egg noodles, creamy polenta . . . or whatever you'd like—this pork is great with any carb

Sprinkle the pork pieces all over with the salt. Let sit at room temperature for an hour before cooking if you have the time (if not, it's okay to skip this step—it just helps the meat cook more evenly and allows the salt to get in there a bit more).

Place the oil in a large heavy pot (such as a Dutch oven) over medium-high heat. Add the pork pieces and cook, turning them as each side browns, until browned all over, about 10 to 15 minutes total.

Add the chicken broth, bay leaves, apricots, olives, and rosemary to the pot. Cover, turn the heat to low, and simmer gently until the pork is incredibly tender, about 2½ hours.

Remove the pot from the heat and use tongs or two forks to shred the pork directly in the pot (discard any large pieces of fat as you work). Then mix the shredded pork together with all the juices in the pot and season to taste with salt.

Serve hot with the carb of your choosing.

FOR THE LOVE OF BETTER THAN BOUILLON

If there's just one thing I hope you take away from this book, it is this: don't be afraid to make things easier for yourself wherever you can. In my kitchen, the best example of this is my love of Better Than Bouillon, a paste that you can whisk into boiling water to create instant broth (or add directly to soups, stews, etc., for extra flavor). If I had a dollar for each time I've mentioned it in my cooking classes, I'd have a lot of dollars. Let me clarify that this is not a sponsored essay: I just love the stuff and think it's a great example of cooking smarter, not harder.

I also want to tell you about some of the other ingredients and tools I depend on to make my life as a home cook easier, but just give me one more minute to explain my love of BTB. Yes, sometimes I make my own stock after I've roasted a chicken or whatever, but nine times out of ten, I use Better Than Bouillon, either their Roasted Chicken Base or, if I'm cooking for anyone vegetarian or vegan, their Seasoned Vegetable Base (I also really like their Vegetarian No Chicken Base, Roasted Garlic Base, and Mushroom Base). I think all these taste great, but I also love the control they offer. I can add just as much paste as I want so I can really season whatever I'm cooking to taste. I also love BTB for practical reasons: it stores easily in its jar and takes up way less space than multiple boxes or cans of broth, plus there's less packaging to recycle. Pro tip: instead of whisking the paste into a measuring cup of water, just add the measured water to whatever you're cooking (soup, stew, etc.), stick your clean whisk into the jar of paste and eyeball what you need, and then just whisk it into the pot (this way you don't have to wash a measuring cup, which honestly isn't a big deal, but I live for these kinds of tiny time-savers).

Okay, on to other ingredients! Life is too short to make homemade puff pastry unless that's your idea of fun (it's not mine, but one of my ideas of fun is lifting heavy weights at the gym, so you decide who you want to listen to). I swear by frozen puff pastry for quick pastries and pot pies. Dufour is my favorite brand (it's made with all butter), but Pepperidge Farm (no butter, just vegetable oil, making it a good option for dairy-free folks) is great too. Speaking of Pepperidge Farm, their refrigerated piecrust is excellent, and it's what I use for the Roasted Chicken Pot Pie on page 246—I like making piecrust, but honestly, no one can really tell the difference.

While we're talking about what I keep in my freezer, can I just say how much I love frozen fruit and many vegetables? They're cleaned, peeled, chopped, and ready to go! They're sitting there waiting for you, but they're not wilting or rotting. They're always picked ripe, so they taste great once you defrost or cook them. They're often cheaper than their fresh counterparts. And they make me feel like I've always got something good to eat. So many things in my cupboard also save me time and energy. Canned beans, canned tuna, etc.

As for tools, well, it turns out I just love a small appliance. I love my Ninja Nutri-Blender—dare I say, more than my Vitamix? It's rare that I am trying to blend more than a couple of cups of liquid at a time, and it's just so much easier to use and clean the smaller blender when I'm making smoothies, salad dressings, pesto, and the like. I use an electric teakettle not just for hot drinks, but also to bring a bunch of water to a boil more quickly than my stove does and then pour it into a pot to cook a little pasta or blanch some vegetables. I like my electric pressure cooker just fine: I wouldn't be upset if it got lost (not sure how that would happen?), but I'm happy I have it for cooking dried beans and making Passover brisket more quickly. I also really love it for cooking rice (for perfect white rice: rinse your rice and then mix equal parts rice and water, season with salt, and cook on high pressure for

3 minutes; do a natural release for 10 minutes, then do a quick release).

And I haven't even mentioned one of the true loves of my life: my air fryer. Using it has made my day-to-day cooking (which means my day-to-day life) easier. Let's get this out of the way: the term "air fryer" is both marketing genius and very misleading. An air fryer does not fry anything. It's a compact countertop convection oven. The key to loving your air fryer, at least for me, is not expecting it to fry anything, but embracing what it can do well: cook things, especially vegetables, very fast and get them nice and brown without heating up your kitchen or leaving a lot of stuff to clean up. When people ask me whether they should get one, I say if you have enough extra counter space and you're not regularly cooking for a lot of people, it's worth a shot (you can't cook a large quantity of food at one time in it, so it's probably not the greatest thing if you're cooking for a large household).

I cook almost everything the same way in the air fryer: I coat whatever I'm cooking with a little olive oil, season with kosher salt, and cook it on the "AirFry" function set to 400°F for about 15 minutes, being sure to shake the basket halfway through cooking. I make some of the best crispy roasted potatoes I've ever had this way (just FIFTEEN MINUTES TO CRISPY POTATOES!). I also use it for broccoli, squash, sweet potatoes, cauliflower, green beans, Brussels sprouts, fish, and meatballs. Basically anything that doesn't have to be cooked in liquid (soups, pasta, rice, braised dishes, etc.).

Reading about these ingredients and tools might make it seem like I don't actually love to cook. Quite the opposite! I love to cook so much, but I also know, and experience, how much labor it is to cook every single day. So I rely on these items to make my love of cooking sustainable. I don't have to be a hero in my kitchen. I just want to make something good to eat.

SECTION FOUR:
RICE, MORE GRAINS & PASTA

ONE-POT RICE DISHES

I love a one-pot meal not only for its ease and coziness, but also (especially?) because cleanup is so streamlined. The kind I make most often is some sort of meat-vegetable-rice situation, and I never make it exactly the same way, because it's always a product of whatever I've got on hand. And it's always great. I think of this as an ode to the dishes just about every culture has that stretch some rice into a warm, nourishing meal (pelau, jambalaya, arroz con pollo, mujadara, and on and on).

   To make a one-pot rice dish, sauté some vegetables in oil (could be a chopped onion, could be a jar of kimchi . . . could be anything!), add something substantial (sausage, a can of chickpeas, etc.), and then add 1 cup of white rice and 2 cups of liquid (water, tomato paste plus some broth, just broth, a splash of wine plus some broth . . . the options are limitless). Simmer it all for about 25 minutes, then serve with any topping that gives the rice a little pop—grated cheese, lemon wedges, red pepper flakes . . . dealer's choice.

ONE-POT RICE DISHES	SAUTÉ VEG IN OIL	ADD A SUBSTANTIAL THING	ADD 1 CUP RICE & 2 CUPS OF LIQUID	FINISH/ SERVE WITH
CHORIZO + SOFRITO RICE	ONION, BELL PEPPERS & GARLIC	SPANISH CHORIZO	TOMATO PASTE & CHICKEN OR VEG BROTH	LEMON WEDGES FOR SQUEEZING
CHICKPEA + SPINACH RICE	ONION, GARLIC & SPICES	FROZEN SPINACH + CANNED CHICKPEAS	CHICKEN OR VEG BROTH	FETA & CHOPPED FRESH DILL
CHICKEN + KIMCHI RICE	KIMCHI	CUT-UP CHICKEN	KIMCHI JUICE & CHICKEN OR VEG BROTH	MORE KOREAN RED PEPPER FLAKES
MUSHROOM SWISS BURGER RICE	ONIONS, MUSHROOMS + GARLIC	GROUND BEEF	WORCESTER-SHIRE SAUCE & CHICKEN (OR VEG) BROTH	GRATED GRUYÈRE CHEESE
SHRIMP + BACON RICE	ONION WITH OLD BAY	BACON & SHRIMP	CHICKEN OR VEG BROTH	LEMON WEDGES FOR SQUEEZING

CHORIZO + SOFRITO RICE

If you don't have a food processor to finely chop the vegetables for the sofrito (or don't want to clean one), just finely chop the vegetables by hand. The food processor makes them almost like a salsa, which allows the ingredients to become a sort of amalgam rather than individual pieces (but chunky is fine too!). For the chorizo, I really like the D'Artagnan Spanish-style chorizo, but use whatever you can find—and even better if you can get it from a local source (and feel free to use vegan chorizo!).

Serves about 4

1 large yellow onion, roughly chopped

1 red bell pepper, cored and seeded, roughly chopped

1 green bell pepper, cored and seeded, roughly chopped

6 garlic cloves

¼ cup olive oil

½ pound Spanish-style fully cooked chorizo, cut into ¼-inch-thick coins

2 tablespoons tomato paste

1 teaspoon ground cumin

1 teaspoon sweet pimentón (smoked Spanish paprika)

½ teaspoon cayenne pepper

Kosher salt

1 cup long-grain white rice

2 cups chicken or vegetable broth (or boiling water mixed with Better Than Bouillon)

For serving: 1 lemon, cut into wedges

Place the onion, peppers, and garlic in the bowl of a food processor and pulse until finely chopped (the mixture will resemble salsa). Reserve.

Place the oil in a large heavy pot (such as a Dutch oven) over medium-high heat. Add the chorizo and cook, stirring, until it begins to crisp, about 5 minutes. Add the reserved vegetables, the tomato paste, cumin, pimentón, cayenne, and a large pinch of salt and cook, stirring now and then, until most of the liquid from the vegetables evaporates, 5 minutes or so.

Stir the rice and broth into the vegetables. Turn the heat to high and bring the mixture to a boil, then immediately lower the heat so that the mixture simmers. Season the cooking liquid to taste with salt. Cover the pot and cook until the rice is tender, about 25 minutes. Remove the pot from the heat and let the rice sit, covered, for 10 minutes.

Uncover the pot, give everything a good stir, and season to taste one final time with salt. Serve immediately, with the lemon wedges for squeezing over.

CHICKPEA + SPINACH RICE

This dish is absolutely one of my favorite recipes—so much so that it inspired this section of the book. The combination of onion, garlic, spices, spinach, and chickpeas is just so comforting. I like to serve this as a side dish, especially with a batch of Braised Spiced Lamb Meatballs (page 210). And it's also great on its own as a main dish. Don't forget the feta and dill at the end. They bring a lot of freshness and *pop* to the rice.

Serves about 4 as a main dish, or 6 to 8 as a side dish

¼ cup olive oil

1 large yellow onion, diced

6 garlic cloves, minced

2 teaspoons dried oregano

2 teaspoons ground coriander

1 cup long-grain white rice

One 10-ounce package frozen spinach (no need to defrost)

One 15-ounce can chickpeas, drained and rinsed

2 cups chicken or vegetable broth (or boiling water mixed with Better Than Bouillon)

Kosher salt

For serving: Crumbled feta cheese and chopped fresh dill

Place the oil in a large heavy pot (such as a Dutch oven) over medium-high heat. Add the onion and cook, stirring now and then, until it begins to soften, about 5 minutes.

Add the garlic, oregano, coriander, and rice and stir just to coat the rice with the spices and oil. Add the spinach, chickpeas, and broth, turn the heat to high, and bring the mixture to a boil, then immediately lower the heat so that the mixture simmers. Season the cooking liquid to taste with salt (the exact amount will depend on how salty your broth is). Cover the pot and cook until the rice is tender, about 25 minutes. Remove the pot from the heat and let the rice sit, covered, for 10 minutes.

Uncover the pot, give everything a good stir, and season to taste one final time with salt. Serve immediately, topped with feta and dill.

CHICKEN + KIMCHI RICE

File this under "easiest one-pot meal." By using a big jar of kimchi, you obviously get a ton of flavor, but you also get the benefit of a bunch of cabbage that's already been cleaned and chopped. Like every one-pot rice recipe, this one is really nice topped with fried eggs. You can also add some grated sharp cheddar cheese right before serving (cheddar and kimchi are great friends).

Serves about 4

¼ cup neutral oil (such as vegetable, grapeseed, or canola)

1 pound boneless, skinless chicken breasts or thighs, cut into bite-sized pieces

Kosher salt

2 teaspoons Korean red pepper flakes, plus more for serving

One 16-ounce jar cabbage kimchi, with its juice

1 cup short-grain white rice

2 cups chicken or vegetable broth (or boiling water mixed with Better Than Bouillon)

Place the oil in a large heavy pot (such as a Dutch oven) over medium-high heat. Add the chicken and season with a large pinch of salt and the Korean red pepper flakes. Cook, stirring, until the chicken is firm and browned in spots, about 8 minutes.

Add the jar of kimchi to the pot, juice and all, along with the rice and broth. Turn the heat to high and bring the mixture to a boil, then immediately lower the heat so that the mixture simmers. Season the cooking liquid to taste with salt (the exact amount will depend on how salty your broth is), cover the pot, and cook until the rice is tender, 25 minutes. Remove the pot from the heat and let the rice sit, covered, for 10 minutes.

Uncover the pot, give everything a good stir, and season to taste one final time with salt. Serve immediately, with pepper flakes alongside for sprinkling on top.

MUSHROOM SWISS BURGER RICE

Okay, this is definitely not the most photogenic pot of food, but it tastes amazing and is incredibly satisfying. If you use Better Than Bouillon for your broth (like I do; see page 160), this is a great place to use their mushroom base. If you want to add an extra vegetable moment, throw in a package of frozen spinach when you mix in the rice and broth.

Serves about 4

2 tablespoons olive oil, plus more if needed

1 pound lean ground beef

Kosher salt and freshly ground black pepper

1 large yellow onion, finely diced

½ pound cremini mushrooms, stems trimmed, thinly sliced

2 tablespoons Worcestershire sauce

6 garlic cloves, minced

1 cup long-grain white rice

2 cups chicken or vegetable broth (or boiling water mixed with Better Than Bouillon)

1½ cups grated Gruyère cheese (6 ounces)

Place the oil in a large heavy pot (such as a Dutch oven) over high heat. Add the beef, season with a large pinch of salt and lots of black pepper, and cook, stirring now and then, until just cooked through, about 7 minutes.

If the pot is dry (this will depend on how lean your beef is), add a glug of oil to it. Add the onion and mushrooms, season with a large pinch of salt and a little more pepper, and cook, stirring now and then, until softened a bit and browned in spots, about 10 minutes. Add the Worcestershire sauce and garlic and cook until very fragrant, about 30 seconds.

Stir in the rice and broth. Bring the mixture to a boil, then immediately lower the heat so that the mixture simmers. Season the cooking liquid to taste with salt (the exact amount will depend on how salty your broth is), cover the pot, and cook until the rice is tender, about 25 minutes. Remove the pot from the heat and let the rice sit, covered, for 10 minutes.

Uncover the pot, add the cheese, give everything a good stir, and serve immediately.

SHRIMP + BACON RICE

With all the vibes of a shrimp boil in a simple one-pot rice meal, this gets a ton of flavor from a little bacon and a generous dose of Old Bay Seasoning. If you don't have Old Bay, use ¾ teaspoon each kosher salt, sweet paprika, garlic powder, and celery seeds. All that flavor comes together with the onion, rice, and broth, and then you just lay the shrimp on top after the rice is cooked and the residual heat will cook them perfectly. Serve with cold beer!

Serves about 4

2 tablespoons olive oil

4 slices bacon (about ¼ pound)

1 large yellow onion, diced

1 tablespoon Old Bay Seasoning (see headnote)

1 cup long-grain white rice

2 cups chicken or vegetable broth (or boiling water mixed with Better Than Bouillon)

Kosher salt

1 pound shrimp, peeled and deveined

For serving: 1 lemon, cut into wedges

Place the oil in a large heavy pot (such as a Dutch oven) over medium-high heat. Add the bacon and cook, flipping the pieces now and then, until crisp, about 6 minutes. Transfer the bacon to a plate and reserve.

Add the onion to the bacon fat, season with the Old Bay, and cook, stirring now and then, until the onion is a bit softened and browned in spots, about 5 minutes. Add the rice and broth, turn the heat to high, and bring the mixture to a boil, then immediately lower the heat so that the mixture simmers. Season the cooking liquid to taste with salt (the exact amount will depend on how salty your broth is), cover the pot, and cook until the rice is tender, about 25 minutes.

Uncover the pot and place the shrimp on top of the rice, then cover the pot and let sit off the heat for 10 minutes. The residual heat will cook the shrimp perfectly.

Uncover the pot, crumble the reserved bacon on top of the shrimp, and stir everything well to combine. Serve immediately, with lemon wedges for squeezing over.

GRAIN BOWLS

For satisfying grain bowls that have a little bit of everything you want, start with your choice of grain, anything from rice to grits. Then top with something cooked and soft (garlicky greens, for example), something raw and crunchy (sliced cucumbers or some chopped scallions, say), and something substantial to make it all filling (a fried egg! Halloumi!), and finish with a condiment (could be homemade dressing or just some hot sauce) and a little special something. This last element is what I think really *makes* a grain bowl. It could be some olives, maybe some nuts, maybe pomegranate seeds—just something else that isn't totally necessary and is therefore a little extra memorable. Combined in one happy bowl, these ingredients give you layers of satisfying textures, colors, and flavors.

GRAIN BOWLS	GRAIN BASE
BIBIMBAP (aka The Original Grain Bowl)	WHITE RICE
GREEK ORZO BOWL	ORZO WITH OLIVE OIL
RICE + LENTIL BOWL w/ ALL THE TOPPINGS	50/50 COOKED RICE & LENTILS
SHRIMP + GRITS BOWL	GRITS
CHILD OF THE '90s BOWL	WILD RICE

SOMETHING COOKED & SOFT	SOMETHING RAW & CRUNCHY	SOMETHING SUBSTANTIAL	CONDIMENT	A SPECIAL EXTRA THING
STIR-FRIED CARROTS & SPINACH w/ GARLIC + SESAME OIL	KIMCHI	FRIED EGGS	GOCHUJANG	SCALLIONS & TOASTED SESAME SEEDS
ROASTED EGGPLANT	DICED CUCUMBERS	LOTS OF FETA	PIZZERIA VINAIGRE-TTE	OLIVES
ROASTED SPICED SQUASH	SHREDDED BRUSSELS SPROUTS w/ LEMON + OLIVE OIL	HALLOUMI	TAHINI SAUCE	POMEGRANATE SEEDS
GARLICKY COLLARDS	SCALLION	SAUTÉED SHRIMP	50/50 HOT SAUCE & MELTED BUTTER	COOKED DICED BACON
ROASTED TOMATOES WITH BALSAMIC VINEGAR	BLANCHED GREEN BEANS	CRUMBLED GOAT CHEESE	PESTO	TOASTED PECANS & DRIED CRANBERRIES

BIBIMBAP (AKA THE ORIGINAL GRAIN BOWL)

Translating to "mixed rice" (*bibim* means "mixed" and *bap* means "cooked rice"), Korea's famous bibimbap is the original grain bowl. Note that 1½ cups of uncooked rice will yield 4 generous cups of cooked rice. Of course, cook your rice however you prefer; I like to rinse it, put it in my electric pressure cooker with an equal amount of water, and cook it on high pressure for 3 minutes, then let it release naturally for 10 minutes and end with a quick release. Be sure to stir everything together as you eat, as that's how you get true mixed rice.

Makes 4 bowls

¼ cup neutral oil (such as vegetable, grapeseed, or canola), plus more if needed

2 carrots, peeled, cut into matchsticks

Kosher salt

2 garlic cloves, minced

One 5-ounce container baby spinach

1 teaspoon toasted sesame oil

4 large eggs

4 cups cooked white rice

About 2 cups cabbage kimchi, drained

About ¼ cup gochujang (Korean red pepper paste)

2 scallions, ends trimmed, thinly sliced

4 teaspoons toasted sesame seeds (if yours aren't already toasted, toast them in the dry skillet first, set them aside, and proceed with the recipe)

Place 2 tablespoons of the oil in a large nonstick skillet over medium-high heat. Add the carrots and season with a large pinch of salt. Cook, stirring now and then, until the carrots are a little bit softened and browned in spots, about 5 minutes. Transfer them to a plate and reserve.

If your skillet is dry, add a splash more oil, then add the garlic. Cook, stirring, until the garlic is sizzling and fragrant, about 30 seconds. Add the spinach (it will seem like a ton at first, but once it cooks, it basically disappears) and cook, stirring, until wilted, about 2 minutes. Drizzle over the sesame oil and season with salt. Transfer the spinach to the plate with the carrots (but don't combine them).

One more thing in the skillet! Wipe it out with a paper towel and add the final 2 tablespoons of oil to it. Crack the eggs into the pan and sprinkle each one with a bit of salt. Sprinkle a few drops of water (like a teaspoon total) into the skillet, being sure to let the water hit the bottom of the pan and not the eggs, and immediately cover it with a lid. Let the eggs cook until the whites are cooked through but the yolks are still a bit wobbly, just a minute or two.

Divide the rice among four bowls. Arrange the carrots, spinach, and kimchi in separate sections in the bowls. Place a fried egg on top of each serving and add about a tablespoon of gochujang to each bowl. Sprinkle each bowl with some scallions and a teaspoon of sesame seeds. Serve immediately and encourage your guests to mix everything up before eating!

GREEK ORZO BOWL

A simple combination of roasted eggplant, cucumber, feta, and olives tops this orzo bowl. Chickpeas marinated in extra vinaigrette would be a lovely addition, as would halved cherry tomatoes. If you have an air fryer and want to make this happen even faster, use it to cook the eggplant (cut into cubes, toss with oil and salt, and cook at 400°F for 15 minutes, being sure to shake the basket halfway through).

Makes 4 bowls

1 large eggplant (at least 1 pound), cut into 1-inch cubes

3 tablespoons plus ¼ cup olive oil

Kosher salt

1 pound orzo

1 large cucumber, finely diced

¼ pound feta cheese, crumbled

1 cup pitted kalamata olives (or your favorite olives)

1 batch Pizzeria Vinaigrette (page 24)

Preheat your oven to 425°F. Bring a pot of water to a boil.

Place the eggplant cubes on a sheet pan, drizzle with 3 tablespoons of the olive oil, and sprinkle with ½ teaspoon salt. Use your hands to mix everything together and then spread the eggplant out in an even layer. Roast the eggplant, stirring once or twice along the way, until softened and browned, about 35 minutes. Remove from the oven and reserve.

Meanwhile, salt the boiling water generously and add the orzo to it. Cook until al dente (so *just* soft with a tiny bit of bite to it, not mushy!), usually a minute less than the package tells you the orzo will take. Drain the orzo (a sieve is better than a colander!) and transfer to a large bowl. Drizzle with the remaining ¼ cup olive oil and mix well to combine. Season to taste with salt.

Divide the orzo among four serving bowls. Divide the reserved eggplant, diced cucumber, feta cheese, and olives among the bowls. Serve with the vinaigrette for drizzling on top.

RICE + LENTIL BOWL WITH ALL THE TOPPINGS

My conversation with Palestinian cookbook author Reem Kassis has been one of my favorite podcast interviews. Reem's work reminds me of the way ingredients can connect us to a place even when we can't be there. I think this is one the most powerful roles that food can play: it can bring us home. This recipe combines so many of the flavors from Reem's books in one bowl. It's a lot of steps, but each is easy.

Makes 4 bowls

One 12-ounce package frozen squash

½ cup olive oil

1 teaspoon EACH ground coriander, ground cumin, and sweet paprika

Kosher salt

1 cup brown lentils

1 cup basmati rice

1½ cups chicken or vegetable broth (or boiling water mixed with Better Than Bouillon)

¾ pound Brussels sprouts, thinly sliced

Juice of 1 lemon

2 tablespoons well-stirred tahini

¼ cup boiling water

½ pound Halloumi cheese, sliced

1 cup pomegranate seeds

Place the squash on a sheet pan, drizzle with 2 tablespoons of oil, sprinkle with the spices and a large pinch of salt, and toss everything together. Roast until the squash is tender and browned, about 25 minutes. Set the squash aside.

Meanwhile, place the lentils in a medium saucepan with a large pinch of salt and cover them with water. Bring to a boil, then turn the heat down and simmer, uncovered, until the lentils begin to soften, about 10 minutes. Drain the lentils in a sieve.

Wipe the pan you cooked the lentils in with a dry cloth, add 2 tablespoons of the olive oil to it, and set over high heat. Add the rice and cook, stirring often, until it starts to turn opaque, about 3 minutes. Add the drained lentils and the broth and bring the mixture to a boil, then turn the heat to low, cover, and cook until the rice is tender, about 18 minutes. Remove the pan from the heat and set aside.

Place the Brussels sprouts in a large bowl with 2 tablespoons of oil and half the lemon juice. Massage the lemon and oil into the sprouts to soften them and season to taste with salt.

Place the remaining lemon juice in a small bowl, add the tahini and boiling water, and whisk well to combine. Season to taste with salt.

Place the final 2 tablespoons of oil in a large nonstick skillet and heat over medium-high heat. Add the Halloumi slices and fry until golden on both sides, about 2 minutes per side.

Divide the rice and lentils, squash, Brussels sprouts, and Halloumi among four serving bowls. Drizzle some of the tahini sauce over each serving and top with the pomegranate seeds. Serve immediately.

SHRIMP + GRITS BOWL

Shrimp and grits is one of my favorite Southern dishes. In this version, I shred a bunch of collard greens and sauté them quickly in olive oil and garlic in a skillet while the grits cook slowly on another burner. I move the greens to a bowl, then fry some diced bacon in the same skillet. When it's crispy, I remove the bacon and cook shrimp in the fat it left behind. Once the shrimp are firm (which happens quickly), I finish them with butter, hot sauce, and lemon. By the time all that has happened, the grits are perfectly cooked. In other words, making this recipe is a great lesson in timing all the parts of a dish so they come together. It's like a tiny symphony, and you are the conductor. One quick technical note: to slice the collards, cut out the hard stem from each leaf, pile the leaves on top of each other, roll them tightly into a log, and then cut across into thin slices.

Makes 4 bowls

2½ cups water

2½ cups whole milk

Kosher salt

1 cup white corn grits

2 tablespoons olive oil

2 garlic cloves, minced

1 bunch collard greens, tough stems cut out and discarded, thinly sliced

½ pound bacon, diced

1 pound peeled and deveined shrimp

2 tablespoons unsalted butter

2 tablespoons of your favorite hot sauce

Half a lemon

4 scallions, ends trimmed, thinly sliced

Place the water, milk, and 2 teaspoons salt in a medium saucepan and bring the mixture to a boil over high heat. While whisking, slowly pour in the grits. Turn the heat to low and simmer the grits so that they sputter ever so gently, stirring often to keep them from sticking, until very tender, about 30 minutes.

Meanwhile, place the olive oil in a large nonstick skillet over medium-high heat. Add the garlic and cook, stirring, until sizzling and fragrant, about 30 seconds. Add the collards, sprinkle with a large pinch of salt, add a splash of water (about 2 tablespoons), and cook, stirring now and then, until the collards are softened and bright green, about 2 minutes. Transfer the collards to a bowl and reserve.

Add the bacon to the same skillet and cook over medium heat until browned and crisp around the edges, about 5 minutes. Use a slotted spoon to lift the bacon out of the skillet to a plate, leaving the rendered fat in the skillet.

Add the shrimp to the bacon fat, season with a big pinch of salt, and cook, turning once, until browned on both sides and firm to the touch, about 2 minutes per side. Turn off the heat and add the butter and hot sauce to the skillet; the residual heat will melt the butter. Stir to coat the shrimp in the spicy butter. Squeeze the juice of the lemon half over the shrimp.

Divide the grits among four bowls and then divide the collards, bacon, and shrimp among them. Sprinkle the scallions on top and serve immediately.

CHILD OF THE '90S BOWL

I was born in 1985, and though I started cooking before I was five (truly!), my magnetic pull to the kitchen was really cemented in the 1990s. That means I have a soft spot for foods that were popular then: wild rice, blanched green beans, goat cheese, pecans, dried cranberries, pesto, and balsamic vinegar. This bowl, which combines all those things, feels like a funny, nostalgic ode to my childhood. And, honestly, it holds up.

Makes 4 bowls

2 cups wild rice

6 cups chicken or vegetable broth (or boiling water mixed with Better Than Bouillon)

1 pint cherry tomatoes

2 tablespoons olive oil

2 tablespoons balsamic vinegar

Kosher salt

1 pound green beans, topped and tailed

¼ pound goat cheese, crumbled

½ cup basil pesto (homemade or store-bought)

½ cup toasted pecan halves

½ cup dried cranberries

Preheat your oven to 425°F.

Place the wild rice in a sieve and rinse under cold running water. Transfer the rice to a medium saucepan, add the broth, and bring the mixture to a boil, then turn the heat to low, cover the pan, and cook just until the rice is tender, about 45 minutes. If a little liquid remains, it's okay.

Meanwhile, place the tomatoes, olive oil, balsamic vinegar, and ½ teaspoon salt in a small baking dish, toss to mix, and roast just until the tomatoes soften and burst open, about 25 minutes. Remove from the oven and reserve.

While the tomatoes are roasting, bring a medium pot of water to a boil and salt it generously. Add the green beans and cook until bright green and just barely tender, about 2 minutes. Drain the beans in a colander and rinse under cold water to stop the cooking, then place them on a kitchen towel to dry.

Use a slotted spoon to divide the wild rice among four serving bowls (discard any remaining cooking liquid). Divide the green beans, goat cheese, pesto, pecans, and cranberries among the bowls. Lastly, divide the tomatoes among the bowls and spoon over any juices from the baking dish. Serve immediately.

QUICK PASTAS

As long as there's a package of pasta in our cupboard, I feel like we always have the beginning of something great to eat. To make a quick, easy meal, combine pasta with something juicy (chopped tomatoes, say, or a blended mixture of anchovies, lemon, and olive oil), plus something herby, and then something rich to make it all come together and feel substantial (could be some cheese or spicy, oily breadcrumbs, or even a good old fried egg). Mix and match within these parameters, and you'll always win. With every pasta dish you make, be sure to monitor and taste the pasta as you cook it; the goal is al dente (so *just* soft with a tiny bit of bite to it, not mushy!), usually a minute less than the package directions instruct.

QUICK PASTAS	PASTA SHAPE	JUICY THING	HERBY THING	RICH THING
CAESAR SPAGHETTI	SPAGHETTI	ANCHOVIES, LEMON & OLIVE OIL	CHOPPED FRESH PARSLEY	LOTS OF PARMESAN + (OPTIONAL) FRIED EGGS
FARMERS' LUNCH PASTA	FUSILLI	GARLICKY KALE	CHOPPED FRESH PARSLEY & CHICKPEAS	A SCOOP OF RICOTTA
GRANDMA'S RAW TOMATO ZITI	ZITI	CHERRY TOMATOES WITH GARLIC, BALSAMIC & OLIVE OIL	FRESH BASIL	FRESH MOZZ-ARELLA
BEST TUNA MAC SALAD	ELBOW MACARONI	CANNED TUNA & OLIVES	CHOPPED FRESH PARSLEY, ONION & CELERY	MAYO + LEMON JUICE
KINDA SICILIAN SPAGHETTI	SPAGHETTI	SAFFRON-Y RAISINS + CAPERS	CHOPPED FRESH PARSLEY	SPICY BREADCRUMBS, PINE NUTS & RICOTTA SALATA

CAESAR SPAGHETTI

Okay, I love this recipe so much. You blend garlic, a tin of anchovies with their oil, lemon, olive oil, and Parmesan together, use it to dress your spaghetti, and top it all with parsley (and fried eggs, if you'd like). It's all the elements of Caesar salad dressing combined with the joy of hot pasta. Don't be shy with the black pepper! This spaghetti is also amazing topped with Haley's lemony breadcrumbs, aka Haley's Savory Sprinkles (page 118).

Serves about 4

Kosher salt

1 pound spaghetti

2 large garlic cloves

One 2-ounce tin olive oil–packed anchovy fillets (don't drain—you want to use the oil!)

¼ cup fresh lemon juice

¼ cup extra-virgin olive oil, plus 2 tablespoons for the eggs, if making them

¾ cup finely grated Parmesan cheese

Freshly ground black pepper

2 large handfuls fresh flat-leaf parsley leaves (some tender stems are fine!), roughly chopped

4 large eggs (optional)

Bring a large pot of water to a boil and season generously with salt. Add the spaghetti and cook until al dente.

Meanwhile, place the garlic, anchovies with their oil, lemon juice, ¼ cup olive oil, Parmesan, 1 teaspoon salt, and ½ teaspoon pepper in the pitcher of a blender or the bowl of a food processor and puree until smooth. Reserve.

When the spaghetti is cooked, scoop out and reserve 1 cup of the cooking water and drain the spaghetti in a colander. Return the cooked spaghetti to the empty pot set over low heat. Add the anchovy mixture, reserved cooking water, and parsley and stir well to combine. Season the spaghetti to taste with more salt and/or pepper if needed. Cook, stirring a couple of times, for a couple of minutes, until most of the liquid has evaporated and the pasta is glossy (the water might seem like a lot at first, but it will come together).

Meanwhile, if you're cooking the eggs, heat the 2 tablespoons olive oil in a large nonstick skillet over medium-high heat. Crack the eggs into the pan and sprinkle each one with a bit of salt and a few grinds of black pepper. Sprinkle a few drops of water (like a teaspoon total) into the skillet, being sure to let the water hit the bottom of the pan, not the eggs, and immediately cover the skillet with a lid. Let the eggs cook until the whites are cooked through but the yolks are still a bit wobbly, just a minute or two.

Divide the spaghetti among four pasta bowls. Top each portion with a fried egg, if you cooked them, and serve immediately.

FARMERS' LUNCH PASTA

When I worked at Long Season Farm (see page 107 for more about this experience), I brought my lunch every day and it was almost always leftovers from dinner the night before. One of my go-to full-circle meals was tons of fresh kale (they grow so much at the farm!) dressed with oil, vinegar, and raw garlic and mixed with hot pasta and a can of chickpeas. Topped with a scoop of ricotta, it's a filling, inexpensive meal that can stretch into tomorrow. My pal Sam, who runs the farm, would be mad at me if I didn't tell you his theory that pasta should come in one-and-a-quarter pound boxes, rather than one-pound, because that is the ideal amount of pasta to cook for two hungry farmers to eat for dinner one night and then have enough left over for lunch the next day. The more you know!

Serves about 4

¼ cup olive oil, plus more for drizzling

2 tablespoons sherry vinegar

2 garlic cloves, minced

Kosher salt

1 pound kale (curly or lacinato), tough stems removed, roughly chopped

One 15-ounce can chickpeas, drained and rinsed

2 large handfuls fresh flat-leaf parsley, finely chopped

1 pound fusilli (or any short pasta, like penne, ziti, bowties, etc.)

1 cup fresh whole-milk ricotta

Freshly ground black pepper

Set a large pot of water on to boil.

Meanwhile, place the olive oil, vinegar, garlic, and ½ teaspoon salt in a large serving bowl and stir well to combine. Add the kale and use your hands to scrunch it all together. Really get in there—don't be shy! Add the chickpeas and parsley, stir, and reserve.

Salt the boiling water generously. Add the pasta and cook until al dente.

Drain the pasta and add it to the bowl with the kale and chickpeas. Stir well to combine (the kale might wilt a tiny bit, which is totally fine). Season to taste with more salt if needed.

Serve immediately (or put however much you want for lunch in a container to take with you) with a scoop of ricotta on top of each portion. Drizzle the ricotta with a little bit of olive oil and season each portion with a pinch of salt and a grind of black pepper.

Long Season Farm during "golden hour" in November 2023 (the exact place where I ate so much Farmers' Lunch Pasta from the previous page!).

GRANDMA'S RAW TOMATO ZITI

I remember my grandmother making this pasta dish all the time when I was a little kid, with tomatoes my grandfather grew in their garden. He loved this so much, and I always think of him when I make it. If you want a little extra peppery vegetable moment, stir in some fresh arugula, or just serve this alongside a simple arugula salad.

Serves about 4

2 pints cherry tomatoes, halved (see below for a tip on how to do this easily)

4 garlic cloves, minced

¼ cup balsamic vinegar

½ cup olive oil

Kosher salt

1 pound ziti (or any short pasta, like penne, fusilli, bowties, etc.)

½ pound fresh mozzarella cheese, torn into small pieces

A handful of fresh basil leaves, torn

Set a large pot of water on to boil.

Place the tomatoes, garlic, vinegar, olive oil, and 2 teaspoons salt in a large serving bowl and stir well to combine. Let this mixture sit while the pasta cooks.

Salt the boiling water generously, add the pasta, and cook until al dente.

Drain the pasta and add it to the bowl with the tomato mixture. Stir well to combine. Season to taste with more salt if needed. Stir in the mozzarella and basil.

Serve immediately, making sure to spoon some of the juices at the bottom of the serving bowl on top of everyone's portion.

Pro tip for cutting a bunch of cherry tomatoes in half quickly and safely: put as many as you can fit in a single layer on a container lid, then top them with a matching lid. Use your nondominant hand to hold that top lid down as if you were pressing the top of a hamburger down and then use your dominant hand to cut all the tomatoes in half with a serrated knife, as if you were cutting a bagel in half. For whatever it's worth, this is the best party trick I know! People are always so excited to see that this is possible.

BEST TUNA MAC SALAD

The best way I know to stretch a box of pasta to feed a crowd, this tuna macaroni salad is packed with some of my favorite ingredients: olives, capers, herbs, lemon! Crunchy things! It's so good and honestly only gets better when it sits in a container in the fridge for a day or two, making it an ideal prepare-ahead staple.

Serves about 6

Three 5-ounce cans solid white tuna, drained

1 cup pitted green olives, preferably Castelvetrano, roughly chopped

One 3.5-ounce jar capers, drained

2 large handfuls fresh flat-leaf parsley, finely chopped

A large handful of fresh dill, finely chopped

1 small red onion, finely diced

4 large celery stalks, finely diced

1 cup mayonnaise

Finely grated zest and juice of 2 lemons

Kosher salt

1 pound elbow macaroni (or any short pasta, like penne, fusilli, ziti, etc.)

Set a large pot of water on to boil.

Place the tuna, olives, capers, parsley, dill, red onion, celery, mayonnaise, lemon zest, lemon juice, and a teaspoon of salt in a large bowl and stir well to combine. Let this mixture sit while the pasta cooks.

Salt the boiling water generously, add the pasta, and cook until al dente.

Drain the pasta in a colander and rinse it with cold water (something I will only ever suggest for pasta salad). Shake the colander to drain the water well.

Add the pasta to the bowl with the tuna mixture and stir well to combine. Serve immediately, or cover, refrigerate, and serve cold (or at room temperature) within the next few days.

KINDA SICILIAN SPAGHETTI

A couple of summers ago, I went to Sicily to join my best friend Cleo on her family vacation. I loved the combination of saffron, raisins, and capers we found in so many dishes there. Inspired by the island, we made a version of this spaghetti together one night months later. Even on a cold winter evening, we were transported back to that incredibly special, sunny place. If you'd like a little extra heft and a deeper savory hit, you can add a tin or two of sardines (break them up as you stir them in), or try finely chopped well-roasted cauliflower if you want extra heft that's vegetarian.

Serves about 4 to 6

½ cup golden raisins

A big pinch of saffron threads

½ cup boiling water

½ cup olive oil

2 teaspoons fennel seeds

1 teaspoon red pepper flakes

1 cup panko breadcrumbs

Kosher salt

1 pound spaghetti

½ cup toasted pine nuts

One 3.5-ounce jar capers, drained

2 large handfuls fresh flat-leaf parsley leaves (some tender stems are fine!), roughly chopped

1 cup coarsely grated ricotta salata (or ½ cup grated pecorino or Parmesan cheese)

Set a large pot of water on to boil. Although this recipe has a lot of steps, everything goes quickly and waiting for the water to boil is the part that actually takes the longest!

Place the raisins, saffron, and boiling water in a small bowl. Set aside.

Place ¼ cup olive oil in a large nonstick skillet over medium-high heat and add the fennel seeds and pepper flakes. Once they begin to sizzle, add the breadcrumbs and cook, stirring now and then, until golden brown, about 3 minutes. Sprinkle with a large pinch of salt, then transfer the fried breadcrumbs to a plate and reserve.

At this point, your big pot of water will likely be boiling; if not, wait until it is! Salt the water generously, add the spaghetti, and cook until al dente. Reserve ½ cup of the pasta cooking water. Drain the spaghetti and return it to the empty pot over medium-high heat. Add the reserved pasta cooking water, plus the raisins and their soaking liquid, and cook just until a little of the liquid has evaporated, about 1 minute. Turn off the heat, add the pine nuts, capers, parsley, half the grated cheese, and half the breadcrumbs, and stir everything well to combine. Season the pasta to taste with more salt if needed.

Transfer the pasta to a serving platter. Drizzle evenly with the remaining ¼ cup olive oil and top with the remaining breadcrumbs and cheese. Serve immediately.

A CONVERSATION WITH MY MOM ABOUT OUR BODIES

I wrote an essay for *Simply Julia* called "On the Worthiness of Our Bodies," which was an honest reflection on my evolving relationship with my own body and how I nourish it. It broke something open for me in a very wonderful way. I had spent my whole career prior to that essay talking about how lovely food is while being very closeted about how much I struggled with an eating disorder.

Sharing this personal story helped me feel so much less alone, so incredibly connected, and so much more able to understand the bigger-than-me systemic issues that fueled my personal struggles. I've been able to see the forest through the trees and connect the dots between white supremacy and diet culture. Meaning I've been able to understand that generations of other-ing most bodies from a very particular idealized type has caused so many of us so much turmoil (though many of us less than others). I've been able to embrace my queer pride as a blueprint for my fat liberation. I've been able to learn from so many others who have been doing this work for so long, people like Sonya Renee Taylor, Dr. Sabrina Strings, Virginia Sole-Smith, Aubrey Gordon, and Da'Shaun L. Harrison.

Over the last few years, I have had many meaningful conversations with other people about how they navigate their own bodies and understand the larger structures at play. Sometimes these conversations have been with strangers on the internet; sometimes they've been tearful, intimate conversations with my closest friends. I've talked to students at the Culinary Institute of America about anti-fatness in the food industry and how to combat it, and I've talked to my doctor about why I no longer wish to be weighed in her office. I have offered "No Judgment" classes, where we gather together online to cook and eat

together and talk about why those things can sometimes feel hard.

One person who has listened to a lot of these conversations is my mother. But we have not actually talked directly about a lot of it, because a few years ago I asked my mother not to talk to me about weight. She honored this request and has been a witness to my evolving understanding of my body. I thought it would be worth picking the conversation with her back up and sharing it here.

Julia: When did your consciousness about your body and weight start? Do you remember?

Rochelle: I have a very clear memory. It was in the second grade. I don't know if I've told you this story or not, but we were all lined up and we got weighed. We were put on a scale and then they wrote our numbers down on the board. I remember mine was higher than other people's. I felt ashamed. Like something was wrong with me and I didn't somehow fit in.

Julia: So it started for you outside of your family?

Rochelle: Yes, but it also started with my older sisters, and I really think it started for them when we got our first television set. I was born in the forties and grew up during the fifties, a time when life was all one-size-fits-all. You ate at a certain time, right after your father walked in the door, took off his coat, and put on a sweater, you know. You were supposed to be a little girl that wore a dress that had a waistline.

Julia: Okay, I'm going to flash forward very fast. You had nearly four decades of navigating your body and feelings about your weight before you

had kids. When you had us and continued to put yourself through so much trying to make yourself smaller, were you conscious that you were doing that at the same time you were raising kids?

Rochelle: This is a really provocative question for me. I think that I was very immature as a parent, obviously not young, but immature in terms of parenting. You parent the way you've been parented, right?

Julia: I'm not sure. But I meant to say something before that I think is important. Which is that I'm not asking this question to blame you.

Rochelle: No, I got that. I'm clear about that.

Julia: I just want to better understand.

Rochelle: You know, I grew up with parents that parented in a certain way. And I think most of the information you get about parenting is from your parents and how they brought you up. The way I was brought up, girls were minimal. We were minimized. We were supposed to get married. And behave in certain ways. My parents weren't reading parenting books. My mother never even learned how to read. I was always looking at other families and thinking they were better. They were more Americanized than I was. Both of my parents were refugees and weren't born in America. I wanted to grow up in an American family. Anyway, when you guys were born, I had a ton of parenting books, but I could never really translate them. I didn't realize so much of it until you were out of the house. So the education came to me, but late. I mean the one thing I will say is that I wish I paid more attention. To even ask the question "How are you feeling?"

Julia: Well, it sounds like you weren't really asked that.

Rochelle: Yeah, I grew up unaware of feelings, as opposed to doings. In our house, you did this, you didn't do that, that was good, this was bad, that was this, this was that. It was transactional, and there were consequences for behavior.

Julia: When I was growing up and was very uncomfortable with my body and my weight, I would come to you and express that. And I feel like the answer was always, "Well, what do you want to do about it?" You'd support me in what I wanted to do about it, but it wasn't ever about what I felt. And it was never about where those feelings came from and that there was nothing wrong with me.

Rochelle: Yeah. Yes. That's a big thing.

Julia: How do you feel about that period now?

Rochelle: All I can do is acknowledge it. My contention is that's the way it was and doesn't mean we have to continue having it be that way. I'm sorry it happened that way.

Julia: I appreciate that. You know, I feel like I had to get to a point where I could have a better relationship with my body that wasn't contingent on whether or not you apologized. And wasn't contingent on how you treated your body. I mean, an apology is worthy and meaningful, but I think right now what feels worthy and meaningful is seeing you start to have a better relationship with your body. It's what I wish had always been the case for both of us.

Rochelle: Well, that goes to your last question you sent me about what do I observe about your relationship with your body now.

Julia: How so?

Rochelle: You know, I smile when I see you and sometimes you say, "What are you smiling at?" And I'm smiling at you. Because you're happy. You're strong. And your posture is great not because of how you stand up, but because you're fully present. And grounded. And it's beautiful. You're absolutely beautiful. To see that, that makes me happy.

Julia: I feel so much less afraid to take up space than I used to.

Rochelle: You take up the space. Seriously, it's wonderful to see all of you.

Julia: A few years ago, I asked you to stop talking about weight with me. Yours, mine, anyone's. How did it feel when I asked you that?

Rochelle: I thought it was interesting. It was a good idea. But I was struck, you know. I just thought, gee, this is a good idea, but I had so much trouble doing it. Was it hard for you as well?

Julia: I don't think I stopped having the conversation in general, but it was hard for me to keep having it with you. It is all very surreal to talk about this now and hear more about how you grew up and were comparing yourself to the other kids in your school, whether it was like the size of your body or how Americanized everyone was. There's a thread of comparison that I'm hearing. Like you trying to figure out how you are in comparison to other people.

Rochelle: Absolutely, absolutely.

Julia: My image of my own body was so negative for so long, and I do think a lot of it for me was figuring out myself in comparison to you. So I had to stop doing that so I could figure out something different.

Rochelle: Yeah.

Julia: So it felt scary to ask you not to talk to me about your weight or my weight anymore. Also because it had also felt like such a bond. To talk to you about our bodies and what we were eating or not eating. I felt such a closeness to you for that.

Rochelle: Thank you. Yeah, thank you. I like hearing that.

Julia: And I didn't want to make you feel bad, but it also felt like continuing that conversation with you was making me feel bad. So I put myself a little bit ahead, which felt scary because I didn't want to hurt you, but I also didn't want to hurt me. But I think ultimately it's been really good.

Rochelle: Well, we sure found other things to talk about!

SECTION FIVE:
MAIN DISHES

MEATBALLS

When dinnertime arrives, I'm never not in the mood for meat-balls. Most meatball recipes include eggs and breadcrumbs, which makes the meat mixture more tender, binds the ingre-dients, and extends the meat so that it can feed more people. But you don't have to use eggs and breadcrumbs as the bind-ing; you can play around with a bunch of different ingredients (once again, this is a great reminder that when we understand why something is in a recipe, we better understand how to play around with that part). The key is to choose things that have some moisture but aren't too wet, like grated zucchini, cooked spinach, or ricotta cheese. It's important to season meatballs generously because, well, they'll taste better! Meatballs can be panfried, roasted on a sheet pan, air-fried, or cooked directly in a sauce or soup. Coat them with a sauce or glaze, or serve alongside a sauce of some kind, whether it's store-bought marinara or a dip made of yogurt, garlic, dill, and lemon. And the best part of making meatballs? Having leftover meatballs! Add them to soup, sandwiches, pizza . . . everything's better with a meatball.

MEAT-BALLS	MEAT	BINDING	SEASONING	SAUCE OR GLAZE
BRAISED SPICED LAMB MEATBALLS	GROUND LAMB	EGGS & BREAD-CRUMBS	LOTS OF SPICES	SWEET-AND-SOUR TOMATO SAUCE
TURKEY MEATBALLS WITH GOCHUJANG GLAZE	GROUND TURKEY	EGG & PANKO	SESAME OIL, SOY SAUCE & FISH SAUCE	GOCHUJANG, HONEY & WATER
BEEF, SPINACH & FETA MEATBALLS	GROUND BEEF	FROZEN SPINACH & FETA	GARLIC POWDER & DRIED OREGANO	YOGURT WITH GARLIC, DILL & LEMON
SPRINGTIME CHICKEN MEATBALLS	GROUND CHICKEN	GRATED ZUCCHINI	FRESH DILL & MINT	LEMONY TAHINI SAUCE
ITALIAN SAUSAGE & RICOTTA MEATBALLS	GROUND PORK & ITALIAN SAUSAGE	RICOTTA CHEESE	PARMESAN, FRESH PARSLEY, SALT & PEPPER	MARINARA

BRAISED SPICED LAMB MEATBALLS

Fragrant with cumin, coriander, and paprika, these meatballs are one of my favorite make-ahead dishes. Everyone loves them, and this is a great way to stretch a pound of ground lamb into a big pot of food. Like all saucy meatballs, these freeze beautifully (freeze in the sauce, defrost in the fridge overnight, and then reheat in a pot over low heat). Serve with rice and a salad or vegetable of your choice.

Makes a dozen meatballs (about 2 to 4 servings, depending on side dishes)

For the meatballs:

2 large eggs

¾ cup breadcrumbs (I use panko, but use what you have—feel free to use gluten-free crumbs)

2 teaspoons EACH ground cumin, ground coriander, sweet paprika, and garlic powder

1 teaspoon kosher salt

1 pound ground lamb (or any type of ground meat, including vegan "ground meat")

Olive oil for cooking

For the sauce:

4 garlic cloves, minced

3 tablespoons tomato paste

One 28-ounce can crushed tomatoes

2 tablespoons brown sugar (or granulated sugar or maple syrup)

2 tablespoons red wine vinegar

Kosher salt

First, make the meatballs: Place the eggs in a large bowl and scramble well with a fork. Add the breadcrumbs, spices, and salt and stir well to combine. Mix in the meat. Divide the mixture into a dozen portions, shaping them into balls (it's easiest to divide the meat mixture in half, then in half again and so on).

Coat the bottom of a large heavy pot (such as a Dutch oven) with a little bit of oil and set it over medium-high heat. Once it's hot, add the meatballs and cook, turning them every so often, until browned all over,

about 10 minutes. (The meatballs don't need to be completely cooked at this point, just browned.) Transfer them to a plate.

Next, make the sauce in the same pot: There should still be some fat at the bottom of your pot; if not, add a glug of olive oil. Add the garlic and tomato paste and cook, stirring, until very fragrant, about 30 seconds. Add the tomatoes and use a wooden spoon to scrape up any stuck-on bits from the bottom of the pot. Bring the tomato mixture to a boil, turn the heat down, and stir in the brown sugar and vinegar. Season the sauce to taste with salt.

Combine the meatballs and sauce: Return the meatballs to the pot, cover, and simmer until the meatballs are completely cooked through and tender, about 20 minutes. Serve hot.

TURKEY MEATBALLS WITH GOCHUJANG GLAZE

These Korean-inspired meatballs are great served with rice, a vegetable or two, and some kimchi. I especially like them with Gingery Baby Bok Choy (page 81) and a pile of sliced cucumbers. You can add some thinly sliced scallions to the meat mix if you'd like a bit more texture and color. You can also substitute any type of ground meat (pork would be especially juicy). Like all meatballs, these are a perfect cocktail snack when made bite-sized. Whether you're enjoying them for your main meal or as an appetizer, you can double the glaze so you will have extra sauce, if you'd like.

Makes 16 small meatballs (about 2 to 4 servings, depending on side dishes)

For the meatballs:
1 large egg

1 tablespoon toasted sesame oil

1 tablespoon soy sauce

1 tablespoon fish sauce

¾ cup panko breadcrumbs

1 pound ground turkey
(preferably dark meat)

Cooking spray

For the glaze:
3 tablespoons gochujang
(Korean red pepper paste; or
substitute sriracha)

3 tablespoons honey
(or maple syrup)

2 tablespoons water

Make the meatballs: Preheat your oven to 400°F. Line a sheet pan with parchment paper.

Place the egg, sesame oil, soy sauce, and fish sauce in a medium bowl and whisk well to combine. Stir in the panko and then mix in the turkey (your hands are the best tool at this point). Divide the mixture into 16 portions, shaping them into balls (it's easiest to divide the meat mixture in half, then in half again and so on), and space them evenly on the sheet pan.

Spray the meatballs with cooking spray and roast until just about firm to the touch, about 15 minutes.

Meanwhile, make the glaze: Place the gochujang, honey, and water in a small bowl and whisk well to combine.

When the meatballs are just firm to the touch, pour the glaze evenly over them and return them to the oven (the glaze will seem liquidy at this point and that's okay; it will thicken in the oven). Continue to roast until the meatballs are totally firm to the touch and the glaze is nice and glossy, about 5 minutes. You can always crack one of the meatballs open to make sure it's cooked through, if you need some reassurance!

Roll the meatballs in the thickened glaze on the sheet pan to coat them and serve hot.

BEEF, SPINACH + FETA MEATBALLS

I often cook these meatballs in my air fryer (400°F for 15 minutes, turning them halfway through cooking), making for an incredibly quick, satisfying meal, but cooking them in the oven is easy too. Serve with warm bread, cooked rice, or orzo, plus a simple salad (like chopped romaine and tomatoes with Pizzeria Vinaigrette, page 24). Or use these for Greek-style meatball sandwiches by tucking them into pita bread with lettuce, tomato, and lots of the yogurt sauce.

Makes a dozen meatballs (about 2 to 4 servings, depending on side dishes)

One 10-ounce package frozen chopped spinach, defrosted, squeezed dry

¼ pound feta cheese, crumbled (about 1 cup)

1 tablespoon garlic powder

1 tablespoon dried oregano

Kosher salt

1 pound ground beef

Cooking spray

One 5-ounce container plain full-fat Greek yogurt

1 small garlic clove, minced

A small handful of chopped fresh dill

1 lemon

Preheat your oven to 400°F. Line a sheet pan with parchment paper.

Place the spinach, feta, garlic powder, dried oregano, and 1 teaspoon salt in a large bowl and stir well to combine. Add the beef and mix well (your hands are the best tool at this point). Divide the mixture into a dozen portions, shaping them into balls (it's easiest to divide the meat mixture in half, then in half again and so on), and space them evenly on the sheet pan. Spray with cooking spray.

Roast the meatballs until browned and firm to the touch, about 25 minutes. You can always crack one open to make sure it's cooked through, if you need some reassurance!

Meanwhile, place the yogurt in a small bowl and whisk in the garlic and dill. Cut the lemon in half and squeeze the juice from one half over the yogurt mixture. Stir in the lemon juice and season the sauce to taste with salt. Cut the remaining lemon half into wedges.

Serve the meatballs hot, warm, or at room temperature, with the yogurt sauce drizzled on top and the lemon wedges alongside for squeezing over.

SPRINGTIME CHICKEN MEATBALLS

Grated zucchini extends a pound of ground chicken into so many meatballs and helps to keep them from drying out. You can use a box grater for the zucchini or the grater attachment on your food processor if you have one (this is especially helpful if you're making more than one batch). For a beautiful meal, serve these on a platter next to a pot of Chickpea + Spinach Rice (page 169).

Makes a dozen meatballs (about 2 to 4 servings, depending on side dishes)

1 pound zucchini (about 2 medium), ends trimmed, coarsely grated

1 pound ground chicken

1 tablespoon garlic powder

A large handful of fresh dill, finely chopped

A large handful of fresh mint leaves, finely chopped

Kosher salt

Cooking spray

3 tablespoons well-stirred tahini

3 tablespoons fresh lemon juice

¼ cup boiling water

Preheat your oven to 400°F. Line a sheet pan with parchment paper.

Place the grated zucchini in the center of a kitchen towel and gather the edges of the towel up around it to form a tight bundle. Wring out the zucchini over the sink, squeezing it as tightly as you can to release all the excess water. Transfer the zucchini to a large bowl and add the chicken, garlic powder, dill, mint, and 2 teaspoons salt. Mix everything together well (your hands are the best tools for this job).

Divide the mixture into a dozen portions, shaping them into balls (it's easiest to divide the meat mixture in half, then in half again and so on), and space them evenly on the sheet pan. Spray with cooking spray.

Roast the meatballs until lightly browned and firm to the touch, about 25 minutes. You can always crack one open to make sure it's cooked through, if you need some reassurance!

Meanwhile, place the tahini, lemon juice, and boiling water in a small bowl and whisk well to combine. Season the sauce to taste with salt (about ½ teaspoon).

Serve the meatballs hot, warm, or at room temperature, with the tahini sauce drizzled on top.

ITALIAN SAUSAGE + RICOTTA MEATBALLS

I think the Turkey and Ricotta Meatballs from *Small Victories* might be the most popular recipe I've ever shared. This recipe goes a step further by using half ground turkey and half Italian sausage meat. I've tried making them with just sausage, but the meatballs were a little too tough—this combination is key for a sausage-flavored meatball that's still tender. If you don't want to chop a thing, leave out the parsley (honestly, it just makes them look nice). If you want to make the meatballs ahead, let them cool, refrigerate them in the sauce, and then just reheat in a pot over medium-low heat or in a baking dish in a 300°F oven. You can also freeze the cooked meatballs in sauce if you want them to keep even longer (defrost overnight in the refrigerator before reheating).

Makes 2 dozen meatballs (about 4 to 6 servings, depending on side dishes)

1 pound fresh Italian sausage links (pork or turkey), casings removed (or just use bulk sausage meat)

1 pound ground turkey (or ground pork)

One 15-ounce container ricotta cheese

½ cup finely grated Parmesan or pecorino cheese, plus more for serving

A large handful of fresh flat-leaf parsley leaves, finely chopped

1 teaspoon kosher salt

½ teaspoon freshly ground black pepper

Olive oil cooking spray

Warm marinara sauce (store-bought or homemade) for serving

Preheat your oven to 425°F. Line a sheet pan with parchment paper.

Place the sausage meat, ground turkey, ricotta, Parmesan, parsley, salt, and pepper in a large bowl and use your hands to mix well to combine. Divide the mixture into 24 portions, shaping them into balls (it's easiest to divide the meat mixture in half, then in half again and so on), and space evenly on the sheet pan. Spray the meatballs with a light coating of cooking spray.

Roast the meatballs until firm to the touch and lightly browned, about 25 minutes. You can always crack one open to make sure it's cooked through, if you need some reassurance!

Serve the meatballs topped with warm marinara sauce (you can also warm your tomato sauce in a pot, add the meatballs, and keep warm over low heat until you're ready to eat).

SAUTÉED CHICKEN DISHES

Because boneless, skinless chicken breasts are so quick-cooking, they are often what I turn to for fast, easy dinners (you can also use boneless, skinless chicken thighs in any of these recipes). Whether I leave the chicken breasts whole or cut them into small pieces, I always season the chicken well and brown it in a hot pan with a little oil, then add something(s) to build more flavor, texture, and color (frozen broccoli, a jar of artichoke hearts, a handful of cashews . . . almost anything). Once the chicken is cooked through, I finish it with something punchy and flavorful like a hit of fresh lime, hot sauce, soy sauce, etc. Following this formula (hot pan, a little oil, seasoning, adding another ingredient, and finishing with something flavorful) means tasty chicken dinners are never boring and always within reach.

SAUTÉED CHICKEN DISHES	COAT CHICKEN WITH...	THEN ADD THIS...	FINISH WITH SOMETHING FLAVORFUL
CHICKEN w/ ARTICHOKES, SUN-DRIED TOMATOES + FETA	GARLIC POWDER, PAPRIKA & DRIED OREGANO	JARRED ARTICHOKE ♡s & SUN-DRIED TOMATOES	FETA
CHICKEN FRANCESE	SEASONED FLOUR & BEATEN EGGS	SLICED LEMONS	WHITE WINE, CHICKEN BROTH, BUTTER & PARSLEY
STIR-FRIED HOISIN CHICKEN & BROCCOLI	SALT & FIVE SPICE POWDER	FROZEN BROCCOLI	HOISIN SAUCE & SOY SAUCE
SPICY CHICKEN WITH LIME & CASHEWS	SALT & PEPPER	CASHEWS	SAMBAL, FISH SAUCE, SOY SAUCE & HONEY
CHICKEN FAJITAS WITH POBLANOS & ONIONS	CUMIN, GARLIC POWDER & PIMENTÓN	PEPPERS & ONIONS	FRESH LIME JUICE

CHICKEN WITH ARTICHOKES, SUN-DRIED TOMATOES + FETA

This quick, tasty dish is a testament to ingredients that come with built-in flavor: here, marinated artichoke hearts, sun-dried tomatoes, and feta cheese. You can season the cut-up chicken a couple of days in advance (just store in a plastic bag in your fridge), which makes putting the dish together extremely fast. Feel free to add some fresh or defrosted frozen spinach to the skillet (or any cooking green) and serve with rice pilaf, couscous, mashed or roasted potatoes, garlic bread, or another carb-y pairing.

Serves about 2 generously

1 pound boneless, skinless chicken breasts, cut into 1-inch cubes

2 teaspoons garlic powder

2 teaspoons paprika

2 teaspoons dried oregano

½ teaspoon kosher salt

2 tablespoons olive oil

One 6-ounce jar marinated artichoke hearts

¼ cup chopped oil-packed sun-dried tomatoes (if your jar contains whole tomatoes, just chop a few!)

1 tablespoon red wine vinegar (or any other type of vinegar)

2 ounces feta cheese, crumbled

Place the chicken in a large bowl and sprinkle over the garlic powder, paprika, oregano, and salt. Use your hands to mix everything together.

Place the oil in a large heavy nonstick skillet over high heat. Add the seasoned chicken and cook, stirring now and then, until it is browned in spots, just firm to the touch, and nearly cooked through, about 7 minutes. Add the artichoke hearts with their brine and the sun-dried tomatoes, and cook, stirring, until the brine has mostly evaporated, about 2 minutes. Stir in the vinegar.

Transfer the chicken to a serving platter (or serve straight from the pan), sprinkle with the feta, and serve immediately.

CHICKEN FRANCESE

This is such a classic Italian-American dish, and I just love it. The egg coating becomes so beautifully golden brown and the perfect texture for the lemony sauce. I taught this recipe in one of my Sunday afternoon cooking classes and it was A HIT. We had it with garlic bread and Italian Chopped Salad (page 34). Such a terrific meal!

Serves about 4

4 boneless, skinless chicken breasts

1 cup all-purpose flour

2 teaspoons garlic powder

2 teaspoons kosher salt

3 large eggs

¼ cup extra-virgin olive oil, plus more if needed

2 lemons, 1 thinly sliced, the other juiced

¼ cup dry white wine (or dry vermouth or additional chicken broth)

¾ cup chicken broth (or boiling water mixed with Better Than Bouillon)

2 tablespoons butter, cut into 4 small cubes

A large handful of fresh flat-leaf parsley leaves (some tender stems are fine!), finely chopped

Place one of the chicken breasts in a large resealable plastic bag and use a meat pounder (or a rubber mallet or the bottom of a small but heavy pot) to pound it until it's about ¼ inch thick. Repeat the process with the remaining chicken breasts.

Place the flour, garlic powder, and salt in a wide shallow bowl and whisk well to combine. Place the eggs in another shallow bowl and whisk well to combine.

Place the oil in a large heavy nonstick skillet over medium-high heat. Dredge the chicken breasts in the seasoned flour and knock off any excess, then dip in the beaten egg, turning to coat completely, letting the excess drip off, and add to the hot oil. Cook, flipping the chicken once, until golden brown and cooked through, about 4 minutes per side. Do this in batches if necessary (adding more oil to the pan if needed); discard any excess flour and eggs (they've done their jobs). Transfer the chicken to a large serving platter.

Add the lemon slices to the fat remaining in the pan and cook, stirring, until a tiny bit softened, about 2 minutes. Add the lemon juice, white wine, and chicken broth and turn the heat to high. Boil, scraping the bottom of the skillet with a wooden spoon to loosen any stuck-on bits, until the liquid has thickened slightly, about 2 minutes. Turn the heat to low and stir in the butter one cube at a time, waiting until each melts and is incorporated before adding the next.

Pour the sauce and sliced lemons over the chicken and sprinkle with the chopped parsley. Serve immediately.

STIR-FRIED HOISIN CHICKEN + BROCCOLI

A fast and easy stir-fry, this chicken gets so much flavor from Chinese five spice and hoisin sauce. If five spice isn't something you normally have on hand, I think it's worth investing in a jar. It's a wonderful and versatile spice blend; you can use it to season any meat before cooking, or add it to baked goods like pumpkin pie (think of it as a more interesting version of pumpkin pie spice). If you can't find five spice, substitute a pinch each of ground cloves, cinnamon, ground ginger, and fennel seeds, plus lots of freshly ground black pepper. You can also just do a ton of freshly ground black pepper and call this "Black Pepper and Hoisin Chicken."

Serves about 2 generously

2 tablespoons neutral oil (such as vegetable, grapeseed, or canola)

1 pound boneless, skinless chicken breasts, thinly sliced

½ teaspoon kosher salt

1 teaspoon Chinese five spice powder

One 10-ounce package frozen broccoli (no need to defrost)

2 tablespoons hoisin sauce

2 tablespoons soy sauce

2 tablespoons water

For serving: A handful of fresh cilantro leaves and/or a sprinkle of toasted sesame seeds (optional)

Place the oil in a large heavy nonstick skillet over high heat. Add the chicken and season with the salt and five spice powder. Cook, stirring now and then, until the chicken is browned in spots and nearly cooked through, about 7 minutes.

Add the broccoli, hoisin, soy sauce, and water to the skillet, stir everything to combine, and let it come to a boil. Then continue to cook, stirring now and then, until the chicken is cooked through, the broccoli is hot, and the liquid has mostly evaporated and become glossy, about 5 minutes.

Transfer the chicken to a serving dish (or serve straight from the pan) and top with the cilantro and/or toasted sesame seeds, if you'd like. Serve immediately.

SPICY CHICKEN WITH LIME + CASHEWS

Okay, I don't want to choose favorites, but of all the recipes in this book, this is probably the one I make most often. I love to use the Thai lime and chili cashews from Trader Joe's, but regular roasted cashews work great too. Serve with rice or noodles and some broccoli, green beans, garlicky greens, or Gingery Baby Bok Choy (page 81) for a meal you'll want to return to over and over.

Serves about 2 generously

3 tablespoons neutral oil (such as vegetable, grapeseed, or canola)

1 pound boneless, skinless chicken breasts, thinly sliced

Kosher salt and freshly ground black pepper

1 lime

1 tablespoon sambal (or other chile paste)

1 tablespoon fish sauce

1 tablespoon soy sauce

1 tablespoon honey (or maple syrup)

⅓ cup roasted cashews (salted or not, up to you), roughly chopped

Place the oil in a large heavy skillet over high heat. Add the chicken and season generously with salt and pepper. Cook, stirring now and then, until the chicken is browned in spots and just cooked through, about 7 to 9 minutes.

While the chicken is cooking, use a Microplane or similar tool to finely zest the lime. Place the zest in a small bowl (reserve the lime) and stir in the sambal, fish sauce, soy sauce, and honey.

Add the sambal mixture and cashews to the chicken and stir everything well. Give it all just an extra minute of cooking to allow the sauce to really make its way around every piece of chicken.

Cut the zested lime in half, squeeze the juice over the chicken, and serve immediately.

Every time I make these fajitas, Grace says, "I love this dinner," and there's no better endorsement I can think of. Made with well-seasoned chicken, peppers, and onions all cooked in a hot skillet, the meal is rounded out with things you don't have to cook, just assemble. Serve with warm flour tortillas, lime wedges, hot sauce, sour cream, shredded lettuce, and/or guacamole . . . whatever you want, really.

You can turn this into a sheet pan dinner, if you'd like. Coat the peppers and onion with oil and salt, spread out on a sheet pan, and put the seasoned chicken on top of that bed of vegetables. Roast at 425°F until everything is cooked (about half an hour). You won't have the same charred flavor that the skillet gives, but it's an easy option.

Serves about 4

1½ pounds boneless, skinless chicken breasts, cut into strips

2 teaspoons ground cumin

2 teaspoons garlic powder

1 teaspoon sweet pimentón (smoked Spanish paprika)

Kosher salt

¼ cup neutral oil (such as vegetable, grapeseed or canola), plus more if needed

1 bell pepper (any color), cored and seeded, cut into thin strips

1 poblano pepper, stemmed and seeded, cut into thin strips (or just use a green bell pepper)

1 small white onion, thinly sliced

1 lime, halved

For serving: Warm flour tortillas, plus whatever toppings you'd like

Place the chicken in a large bowl and sprinkle with the cumin, garlic powder, pimentón, and 1 teaspoon salt. Rub the spices all over the chicken.

Place the oil in a large heavy skillet, preferably cast iron, and turn the heat to medium-high. Add the peppers and onion and sprinkle with a large pinch of salt. Cook, stirring NOT TOO OFTEN, until the vegetables are charred in spots and starting to soften, about 10 minutes. Transfer to a bowl; reserve.

Add just enough of the chicken to the skillet to avoid crowding the pan (you will likely need to do this in 2 batches). Cook, stirring now and then, until the chicken is cooked through and browned in spots, about 7 minutes. Transfer the cooked chicken to the bowl with the vegetables and repeat with the remaining chicken, adding more oil to the skillet as needed.

Once all the chicken is cooked, return all of it and the vegetables to the skillet and stir everything together (if everything has cooled down a lot, heat it through before serving). Squeeze the lime halves over everything. Serve immediately, with warm tortillas and whatever toppings you most love.

SHEET PAN DINNERS

People often ask me for sheet pan dinner recipes, and I get it—they're the ultimate in hands-off cooking and multitasking. Throw everything for one meal in the oven and cook all at once? Yes, please. As you'll see in these five recipes, a sheet pan meal can go in so many directions and is an easy way to accommodate a variety of dietary parameters. In general, I like to combine a main thing with a side thing, cover it all with lots of flavor, and then serve it with some greens or grains to round it all out. It really doesn't get much easier.

SHEET PAN DINNERS	MAIN THING	SIDE THING	FLAVOR	FINISH/ SERVE WITH
EGGPLANT PARM HEROES	BROILED EGGPLANT TOPPED WITH TOMATO SAUCE & CHEESE	GARLIC BREAD	BUILT INTO EGGPLANT & GARLIC BREAD	FRESH BASIL AND/OR ARUGULA
EVERYTHING-BAGEL SALMON + SMASHED POTATOES	SALMON	BOILED & SMASHED POTATOES	MUSTARD & EVERYTHING-BAGEL SEASONING	LEMON WEDGES
ROASTED FISH + CAULIFLOWER WITH SICILIAN TOMATO SALAD	COD OR ANOTHER FIRM WHITE FISH	CAULIFLOWER FLORETS	OLIVE OIL, SALT & PEPPER	SICILIAN TOMATO SALAD
BBQ TOFU & SWEET POTATO FRIES	TOFU	SWEET POTATO FRIES	BBQ SAUCE	SLAW!
STICKY PORK WITH BROCCOLI	PORK TENDERLOIN OR BONELESS PORK CHOPS CUT INTO SMALL PIECES	BROCCOLI	STICKY SAUCE (GARLIC, KETCHUP, ETC.)	RICE

EGGPLANT PARM HEROES

I love these. They're incredibly satisfying and require very little cleanup. To make them, you line a sheet pan with foil, cover it with the sliced eggplant, and broil until the eggplant is browned. Then add some tomato sauce (store-bought is fine!) and mozzarella, stick the pan back under the broiler, and boom: low-effort eggplant Parm. While that's all happening, spread some garlic butter on rolls and then broil those too, so you end up with delicious garlic bread for your sandwiches. These heroes give you all the flavor and crunch of breaded eggplant without having to do the work of breading and frying (which is so much labor and so much to clean up). Serve with lots of napkins!

Makes 4 sandwiches

For the eggplant:
1 large eggplant, ends trimmed, cut into ¼-inch-thick slices

Olive oil cooking spray

Kosher salt

2 cups of your favorite tomato sauce (mine is Rao's)

2 cups shredded low-moisture mozzarella cheese

½ cup finely grated Parmesan cheese

For the garlic bread:
4 tablespoons (½ stick) unsalted butter, at room temperature

2 large garlic cloves, minced

1 teaspoon garlic powder

½ teaspoon kosher salt

4 ciabatta rolls (or your preferred hero rolls)

For serving: Fresh basil leaves and/or arugula

Cook the eggplant: Preheat your broiler to high and set your oven rack so it's about 6 inches below the heating element.

Line a sheet pan with aluminum foil (this saves you on cleanup!!! DO NOT USE parchment, as it would *catch fire* under the broiler . . . you don't want that!).

Spray the eggplant slices on both sides with cooking spray and sprinkle evenly with a little salt. Broil, turning once, until nicely browned on both sides, about 2 to 5 minutes per side (keep a close eye on this—the time depends on the strength of your broiler). Remove the pan from the oven.

Spread the sauce over the broiled eggplant, sprinkle the mozzarella evenly on top, and sprinkle the Parmesan evenly on top of that. Place the sheet pan back in the oven and broil until the sauce is bubbling and the cheese is melted, about 5 minutes.

Prepare the garlic bread: Place the melted butter, garlic, garlic powder, and salt in a bowl and stir well to combine. Cut the rolls in half. Spread the butter mixture evenly over the cut sides of the bread. Lift the foil holding the cheesy eggplant off the sheet pan and set it on your counter, then use the empty sheet pan for the garlic bread (or just use a different sheet pan). Place the roll halves butter side up on the sheet pan and broil until the rolls are warm and lightly browned, even a little crisp, about 2 minutes.

Divide the eggplant mixture among the rolls, add some fresh basil and/or arugula to each sandwich, and serve.

EVERYTHING-BAGEL SALMON + SMASHED POTATOES

This is one of the easiest ways I know to cook salmon—just slather it with mustard and cover it with everything-bagel seasoning. Coupled with smashed potatoes, it's a perfect meal. I like to use Trader Joe's Everything But the Bagel Sesame Seasoning, but you can find a similar blend just about anywhere, from Costco to Aldi. You can also make your own by mixing a teaspoon each of kosher salt, poppy seeds, black sesame seeds, white sesame seeds, onion flakes, and garlic flakes. But if the previous two sentences stress you out, you can just use 2 tablespoons sesame seeds and call this "Sesame Salmon." Both the salmon and potatoes are delicious served with sour cream or tartar sauce.

Serves about 4

1 pound small creamer potatoes

¼ cup olive oil

½ teaspoon kosher salt

1 teaspoon garlic powder

1½ pounds salmon, preferably in one large piece (skin-on or skinless)

¼ cup Dijon mustard

2 tablespoons everything-bagel seasoning

For serving: 1 lemon, cut into wedges

Preheat your oven to 400°F. Line a sheet pan with parchment paper.

Place the potatoes in a saucepan and cover with an inch of cold water. Bring the water to a boil over high heat, then turn the heat down and simmer until the potatoes are tender (test with a paring knife), about 15 minutes. Drain the potatoes and transfer them to the sheet pan.

Use the bottom of a mug to press on the potatoes so they crack open and are about ½ inch thick. If some break apart, it's okay! Drizzle the potatoes with the olive oil and sprinkle evenly with the salt and garlic powder.

Spread the potatoes out around the perimeter of the pan so that they make a sort of frame around the open center. Place the salmon in the center of the pan and coat it evenly with the mustard and then the everything-bagel seasoning.

Roast until the potatoes are crisp and the fish flakes easily and is opaque in the center (test by poking it with a paring knife), about 20 to 25 minutes.

Serve with the lemon wedges for squeezing over.

ROASTED FISH + CAULIFLOWER WITH SICILIAN TOMATO SALAD

On the same trip that inspired Kinda Sicilian Spaghetti (page 200), my friends Cleo, Amelia, and I made this for dinner one night in an attempt to use up stray bits of vegetables and herbs in the refrigerator (the celery is key!). We all loved it, and each time I make it now, I'm reminded of one of the most fun vacations I've ever been on. To complete the meal, serve with bread or pasta and a simple arugula salad or some sautéed greens.

Serves about 4

1 large cauliflower, cut into large florets

About ½ cup olive oil

Kosher salt and freshly ground black pepper

1 pound cod fillets (or any firm white fish)

1 pint cherry tomatoes, halved (see page 196 for a tip on how to do this quickly)

1 small garlic clove, minced

2 large celery stalks, finely diced

½ cup pitted green olives, preferably Castelvetrano, roughly chopped

A large handful of fresh basil leaves, roughly chopped

A large handful of fresh flat-leaf parsley leaves (some tender stems are fine!), roughly chopped

2 tablespoons red wine vinegar

Preheat your oven to 400°F. Line a sheet pan with parchment paper.

Place the cauliflower on the sheet pan, drizzle with 2 tablespoons of the oil, sprinkle with a large pinch of salt, and grind over a bit of pepper. Mix everything well with your hands and then spread the cauliflower out so it's in a single even layer.

Roast until the cauliflower begins to soften and brown in spots, about 15 minutes.

Take the sheet pan out of the oven and spread the cauliflower out around the perimeter of the pan so that it makes a sort of frame around the empty center. Place the fish in the center of the pan, drizzle with about 2 tablespoons of the oil, and season generously with salt and pepper.

Return the sheet pan to the oven and continue to cook until the cauliflower is browned and the fish is opaque and flakes easily when pierced with a paring knife or fork, about 15 minutes (or a little more if your fish is thick).

While everything is roasting, place the tomatoes in a bowl and add the garlic, celery, olives, herbs, vinegar, and remaining ¼ cup olive oil. Season generously with salt and pepper.

Transfer the cauliflower and fish to a serving platter (or serve straight from the sheet pan), spoon the tomato salad on top, and serve immediately.

BBQ TOFU + SWEET POTATO FRIES

One of my favorite quick-and-satisfying dinners (that happens to be totally vegan, just FYI), this sheet pan meal features tofu and sweet potatoes that are seasoned with a generous amount of garlic, smoky pimentón, and salt and then the tofu is glazed with barbecue sauce. I like to serve it with a simple cole-slaw or some quickly sautéed collard greens. It's also great with buttered corn on the cob.

Serves about 2 generously

One 14-ounce package extra-firm tofu, cut into 8 planks (each about ½ inch thick)

1 pound sweet potatoes (2 medium or 1 very large), cut into ½-inch-thick fries

2 tablespoons olive oil

1 teaspoon garlic powder

1 teaspoon sweet pimentón (smoked Spanish paprika)

1 teaspoon kosher salt

½ cup barbecue sauce (homemade or store-bought; my favorite is Sweet Baby Ray's)

Preheat your oven to 400°F.

Place the tofu planks on one side of a clean kitchen towel and fold the towel over the tofu (or use a double layer of paper towels). Place a sheet pan on top of the towel-covered tofu and put something heavy on top to gently press the tofu down. Let this setup sit while you slice and season your sweet potatoes.

Place the sweet potatoes in a large bowl and add the olive oil, garlic powder, pimentón, and salt. Use your hands to mix everything well.

Remove the heavy thing from the sheet pan and place the oiled and seasoned sweet potatoes on the pan, spreading them out into an even layer.

Place the pressed tofu in the bowl you used for the sweet potatoes (no need to clean it). Add the barbecue sauce and use your hands to gently coat the tofu with sauce (if some of the planks of tofu break, it's okay). Add the tofu to the sheet pan, trying your best to keep everything in an even layer.

Roast the tofu and sweet potatoes, flipping the pieces over halfway through cooking, until the sweet potatoes are tender and everything is nicely browned, about 40 minutes. Serve.

STICKY PORK WITH BROCCOLI

Tossing cubes of pork and big pieces of broccoli with a sweet-salty-kinda-spicy sauce and roasting them together yields a simple, irresistible dinner. If the sauce seems familiar, it's because I adapted it from the sauce for the Sticky Chicken in *Simply Julia*. You could use chicken or tofu instead of the pork, and feel free to use frozen broccoli instead of fresh (or any firm green vegetable for that matter, such as green beans or Brussels sprouts). Serve with cooked rice.

Serves about 2 very generously

1 pound pork tenderloin or boneless pork chops, trimmed of excess fat, cut into 1-inch pieces

1 pound broccoli, cut into large florets (or frozen broccoli; no need to defrost)

2 tablespoons olive oil

½ teaspoon kosher salt

3 tablespoons ketchup

2 tablespoons honey (or maple syrup)

2 tablespoons soy sauce

1 to 2 tablespoons chile-garlic sauce (such as sambal), or your favorite hot sauce

2 garlic cloves, minced

1 teaspoon cornstarch

Preheat your oven to 425°F.

Place the pork and broccoli on a sheet pan, drizzle with the oil, and sprinkle with the salt. Mix everything well with your hands and then spread it all out so it's in a single even layer.

Roast until the pork is just opaque and the broccoli is bright green, about 8 minutes. Use a paper towel to collect any excess cooking juices from the pan (discard the paper towel).

Meanwhile, mix the remaining ingredients together in a small bowl.

Drizzle the sauce over the pork and broccoli and toss well to combine. Return to the oven and roast until everything is bubbling and glazed, about 10 more minutes. It should all look irresistible! Eat immediately.

SAVORY PIES

I love savory pies, especially when hosting, because they're not things people often make for themselves. Plus, savory pies can usually be made ahead, or at least assembled ahead, and then popped into the oven right before serving. Combining the filling ingredients with some kind of sauce (could be a gravy, could be crushed tomatoes) and then topping it with something wonderfully carb-y (piecrust, mashed sweet potatoes, polenta . . . you get the idea!) is all you need for a perfect pie. Play around with these three main elements—filling, sauce, topping—to find your favorite combinations. Savory pies are also a great place to repurpose leftovers and transfer them into an entirely new dish.

SAVORY PIES	SUBSTANTIAL PART OF FILLING	SAUCE PART OF FILLING	TOPPING
ROASTED CHICKEN POT PIE	SHREDDED ROTISSERIE CHICKEN, PEAS & CARROTS	A SIMPLE GRAVY (BUTTER, FLOUR & BROTH)	STORE-BOUGHT PIE CRUST (OR PUFF PASTRY)
WHITE BEAN, ROASTED TOMATO + POLENTA PIE	WHITE BEANS, FETA & OLIVES	ROASTED CHERRY TOMATOES & OLIVE OIL	POLENTA CIRCLES & PARMESAN
LENTIL & SWEET POTATO SHEPHERD'S PIE	COOKED LENTILS & ONIONS	CRUSHED TOMATOES	MASHED SWEET POTATOES
BLACK BEAN + CHEDDAR CORNBREAD PIE	BLACK BEANS, ONIONS, PEPPERS & SPICES	TOMATO PASTE & CRUSHED TOMATOES	CORNBREAD WITH LOTS OF CHEDDAR
BISCUITS & GRAVY PIE	SAUSAGE, PEPPERS & ONIONS	A SIMPLE GRAVY (BUTTER, FLOUR + MILK)	BUTTERMILK BISCUITS

ROASTED CHICKEN POT PIE

This pot pie looks and tastes like it requires much more effort than it actually does. You can assemble the pie up to a couple of days in advance and bake just before serving (or bake it ahead and warm it up in a 300°F oven). It freezes well too. Either freeze it unbaked and bake from frozen (it will take about an hour), or bake it and just rewarm it from frozen (more like 40 minutes).

Serves about 4

4 tablespoons (½ stick) unsalted butter

1 small yellow onion, finely diced

2 garlic cloves, minced

Kosher salt and freshly ground black pepper

¼ cup all-purpose flour

2 cups chicken broth (or boiling water mixed with Better Than Bouillon)

1 store-bought rotisserie chicken

One 16-ounce package frozen mixed vegetables (peas, corn, and carrots; no need to defrost)

¼ cup heavy cream (optional)

One 9-inch piecrust (homemade or store-bought, or use one sheet of puff pastry), defrosted if frozen

1 egg, beaten

Preheat your oven to 375°F.

Melt the butter in a medium saucepan over medium heat. Add the onion, garlic, 1 teaspoon salt, and ½ teaspoon pepper and cook, stirring now and then, until the onion is just softened but not browned, about 8 minutes.

Add the flour and stir well to combine. Let the mixture cook, stirring often, until it turns the color of a milky cup of coffee, about a solid 5 minutes. While whisking constantly, slowly pour in the broth. The mixture will seem very loose at first, but trust in the power of flour. Bring it to a boil, then lower the heat and simmer, stirring now and then, until slightly thickened, about 5 minutes.

Meanwhile, remove all the meat from the chicken and shred it; discard the skin and bones (or reserve for stock). Add the chicken, mixed vegetables, and cream, if using, to the gravy and stir well to combine. Season to taste with salt and pepper (don't be shy).

Transfer the mixture to a 10-inch pie dish and cover with the piecrust (if using puff pastry, cut the sheet to fit over the pie dish and cover the filling with it). Pinch the edges of the crust against the pie dish to keep it in place. Brush the crust with the beaten egg (you won't use the whole egg—save the rest for your next omelet or batch of scrambled eggs, if you'd like!). Use a paring knife to cut a few slits in the crust so that steam can escape. Sprinkle the crust with a large pinch of salt and a few grinds of black pepper.

Place the pie on a sheet pan (this makes it much easier to get it in and out of the oven) and bake until the crust is browned and the filling is bubbling, about 50 minutes. Serve hot.

WHITE BEAN, ROASTED TOMATO + POLENTA PIE

This pie comes together very quickly, especially if your grocery store stocks precooked polenta in a tube (most do). If not, no worries, just pivot to making your own creamy polenta and topping the pie with that (either pour it on while it's hot and still creamy, or let it chill and then cut into slices and use those; either way is okay!). To round out the meal, serve this with a simple green salad—I like peppery arugula tossed with lemon and olive oil—and lots of bread to sop up the juices in the baking dish. You can also make this in individual ramekins if you want to be extra-adorable (divide the filling between 5- or 6-ounce ramekins, top each with a round of polenta, and bake according to the same directions).

Serves about 4 generously

½ cup olive oil, plus more for drizzling

Two 15-ounce cans white beans, drained and rinsed

1 pint (2 cups) cherry tomatoes, halved (see page 196 for a cool trick!)

6 garlic cloves, minced

Kosher salt

1 teaspoon dried oregano

¼ pound feta cheese, crumbled (just omit for a vegan version)

A large handful of pitted olives (whatever type you like; optional)

One 18-ounce tube precooked polenta, sliced into ¼-inch-thick slices

¼ cup finely grated Parmesan cheese

Preheat your oven to 425°F.

Place the olive oil, beans, tomatoes, garlic, salt, oregano, feta, and olives, if using, in a 9-by-13-inch baking dish (or anything similarly sized that can go in the oven). Use your hands to mix everything well.

Place the polenta rounds on top of the mixture, then drizzle each one with a little olive oil and sprinkle with a small pinch of salt. Sprinkle the Parmesan evenly on top of everything. Bake until the tomato-and-bean mixture is bubbling and the polenta is lightly browned and slightly crisp, about 45 minutes.

Serve warm.

LENTIL + SWEET POTATO SHEPHERD'S PIE

Patiently panfrying the onions in plenty of olive oil is the key to building slow-cooked flavor in this wonderfully savory vegan pie. Serve with a simple green salad or try torn radicchio dressed with Creamy Mustard Dressing (page 26). If you have any leftovers, stir them together with an equal amount of vegetable stock and, voilà, you'll have a beautiful lentil and sweet potato soup!

Serves about 4 to 6

3 pounds sweet potatoes (about 4 large potatoes)

1 cup brown lentils

Kosher salt

¼ cup olive oil

2 large red onions, thinly sliced

2 teaspoons ground coriander

2 teaspoons sweet pimentón (smoked Spanish paprika)

Freshly ground black pepper

One 15-ounce can crushed tomatoes

1 cup full-fat coconut milk

Preheat your oven to 400°F.

Pierce each sweet potato a couple of times with a paring knife or a fork and bake on a foil- or parchment-lined sheet pan until very tender (test with a paring knife), about 1 hour. Let the sweet potatoes sit until cool enough to handle.

Meanwhile, place the lentils and a tablespoon of salt in a medium saucepan and cover the lentils with 2 inches of cold water. Bring the water to a boil, then turn the heat down and simmer, uncovered, until the lentils are just tender, about 25 minutes. Drain the lentils in a sieve and reserve.

While the sweet potatoes roast and rest and the lentils cook, place the oil in a large heavy pot (such as a Dutch oven) over medium-high heat. Add the onions and cook, stirring now and then, until they are very soft and very browned, about 20 minutes.

Add the coriander, pimentón, 1 teaspoon salt, and ½ teaspoon pepper to the onions and stir until the spices become very fragrant. Add the crushed tomatoes and bring the mixture to a boil, then turn off the heat and stir in the lentils. Season the mixture to taste with more salt and/or pepper if needed.

When the sweet potatoes are cool enough to handle, peel them (discard the skins or snack on them). Mash the sweet potatoes together with the coconut milk in a bowl using a potato masher, or mash together in the bowl of a food processor. Season the potatoes to taste with salt and pepper.

Transfer the lentil mixture to a 9-by-13-inch baking dish (or anything similarly sized that can go in the oven). Dollop evenly with the sweet potatoes and then gently spread the sweet potatoes out to cover. Bake until the filling is bubbling and the top is a little bit browned, about 20 minutes.

Serve hot.

BLACK BEAN + CHEDDAR CORNBREAD PIE

This vegetarian casserole is such a cozy option. If you want to make this ahead, go ahead and bake it, then let it cool completely, wrap it well, and refrigerate for up to a few days, or freeze for longer. Warm it back up in a 300°F oven until piping hot (about half an hour if it's been refrigerated, or an hour if frozen). You can also make this in individual-sized foil trays and freeze them—the perfect thing to bring to someone who might be sick or healing.

Serves about 4 to 6

3 tablespoons olive oil

1 yellow onion, finely diced

1 red bell pepper, cored and seeded, finely diced

Kosher salt

4 garlic cloves, minced

2 teaspoons ground cumin

1 teaspoon sweet pimentón (smoked Spanish paprika)

3 tablespoons tomato paste

Two 15-ounce cans black beans, drained and rinsed

One 15-ounce can crushed tomatoes

2 cups coarsely grated sharp white cheddar cheese (about 8 ounces)

1 cup all-purpose flour

1 cup stone-ground yellow cornmeal

3 tablespoons sugar

2 teaspoons baking powder

2 large eggs

1¼ cups buttermilk

6 tablespoons (¾ stick) unsalted butter, melted

For serving: Sour cream (optional)

Preheat your oven to 400°F.

Place the oil in a large heavy pot (such as a Dutch oven) over medium-high heat. Add the onion and bell pepper and season with a large pinch of salt. Cook, stirring now and then, until the vegetables begin to soften and brown in spots, about 10 minutes.

Add the garlic, cumin, pimentón, and tomato paste and cook, stirring, until everything is very fragrant, about a minute. Add the black beans and crushed tomatoes, stir everything together well, and turn off the heat. Season the mixture to taste with salt.

Transfer the mixture to a 9-by-13-inch baking dish (or anything similarly sized that can go in the oven). Sprinkle 1 cup of the cheese evenly on top; set aside for the moment.

Place the flour, cornmeal, sugar, baking powder, and 2 teaspoons salt in a large bowl and whisk well to combine. Add the eggs, buttermilk, and melted butter and whisk well to combine.

Dollop the cornbread batter evenly over the black bean mixture and then gently spread it over the surface. Sprinkle the top evenly with the remaining cup of cheddar cheese. Bake until the top is dark golden brown, about 30 minutes.

Serve hot, with sour cream dolloped on top, if you'd like.

BISCUITS + GRAVY PIE

This is a hearty and fun brunch (or breakfast-for-dinner) option, and it is especially great for entertaining, because you can prepare it ahead. The gravy can be made, cooled, and refrigerated for up to five days. Right before serving, place the gravy in a baking dish, top with the biscuits, and bake! Serve with coffee and juice. You could also throw in a fruit salad or a green salad to help cut the richness.

Serves about 4 to 6

2 tablespoons unsalted butter

1 pound fresh breakfast sausage links (pork, turkey . . . any type you'd like!), casings removed

1 yellow onion, finely diced

1 red bell pepper, cored and seeded, finely diced

1 green bell pepper, cored and seeded, finely diced

¼ cup all-purpose flour

2 cups whole milk

1 cup chicken broth (or boiling water mixed with Better Than Bouillon)

Kosher salt and freshly ground black pepper

One 16-ounce can refrigerated buttermilk biscuits (or 8 unbaked homemade biscuits!)

Preheat your oven to 350°F.

Place the butter in a large heavy pot (such as a Dutch oven) over medium-high heat. Crumble in the sausage and then add the onion and bell peppers. Cook, stirring now and then and breaking up the sausage a bit, until the sausage is cooked through and the vegetables are softened, about 12 minutes.

Sprinkle the mixture with the flour and stir well to combine. While stirring constantly, slowly pour in the milk and chicken broth. The mixture will seem very loose, but trust in the power of flour (and know the gravy will thicken a lot in the oven). Season to taste with salt and pepper (don't be shy; I like a full teaspoon of each).

Transfer the sausage mixture to a 9-by-13-inch baking dish (or anything similarly sized that can go in the oven). Space the biscuits evenly on top (it's okay if some of the sausage gravy is exposed).

Bake until the biscuits are golden brown and the filling is bubbling, about 20 minutes. Serve immediately.

ON QUEER COOKING

Queer and trans people are—*and have always been*—everywhere, including in kitchens across the world. I am so happy to be a queer person who loves to cook and am grateful to share all of myself in my work. Over the course of many years of publishing cookbooks about the food I cook at home, I've also gotten to share stories about who I cook for. The person I cook for the most is my spouse, Grace. Getting to share about our relationship has allowed me to connect with so many other queer people, not to mention parents and other relatives of queer people, who have shared with me what it's meant for them to see their lives reflected in something as familiar as a cookbook. Normalizing queer love, and the vast connections that come from doing that, continues to be one of the most gratifying parts of my work.

Every Monday, I get to not only think about the queerness of food and cooking, I get to really live it. In September 2022, my pal Emmet Moeller, a personal chef who is queer and trans, and I started a local weekly prepared meal service called Full Fridge Club (Emmet came up with the name and I love it). We cook out of Emmet's commercial kitchen in Kingston, New York, where they also cook for private clients and some other folks use the kitchen space for their businesses too. The kitchen is a sunny, happy, clean, and well-organized space. Most of the crew who works there are trans and/or queer. I am so grateful for this safe, positive, and affirming workplace. It

feels powerful to be part of a business where nobody feels like an exception, and it's nice to show that that is possible.

For Full Fridge Club, every week our team gathers to cook a completely new menu of locally sourced, beautiful dishes that our clients take home and enjoy throughout the week. It's like having a more affordable private chef. We are also committed to mutual aid, and for each paying customer, we put at least one meal into one of the free community fridges in Kingston. In our first year alone, we shared one thousand free meals with the community. This commitment to the people around us feels connected to our queerness.

I look forward to our work every Monday. I get to the kitchen first thing in the morning and roll up my sleeves, and Emmet and I go through our menu and figure out who's doing what. We cook all morning, along with Stephen, Emmet's kitchen manager, and together we package and label the food before we all sit down to a late lunch with Pat, who helps us with our dishes. I take meals to one of the community fridges on my way home. We spend the day troubleshooting, brainstorming, and pivoting. We do not put ourselves or our food in strict boxes. We are able to support our farmer friends and cook for clients who are all so kind. We chat and laugh (and, of course, gossip) all day and listen to music, and it's just great.

My lived experiences of queer cooking are reflected in these pages. In a way, I think this is

the queerest book I've worked on. No, it's not wrapped in a rainbow Pride flag, but the charts are so queer. They're boundless and encourage creativity and expression. They allow me to show you exactly how I am constantly queering cooking, meaning I am constantly asking myself if there are other ways of approaching something. The charts take one thing and show how many different dimensions it can have. They look at conventions and say, ". . . Nah."

This feeling of limitlessness is part of what I love about queerness, both personally and culturally. For me, being a queer person has meant pausing before accepting the norms and expectations laid out in front of me. It's meant thinking critically and creatively about these choices and taking agency in my decisions. Being queer has made my life bigger, fuller, and more connected. I feel this way about loving food too. When I pause to think about it, I realize that the way I approach cooking is just like how I approach gender and sexuality: there's no one right way. And isn't that so wonderful?

Emmet and I having a laugh while telling all our guests (many of them old friends!) about the food we served at Gay Soiréeeee, an epic dinner party we threw in October 2023.

SECTION SIX:
BAKED GOODS

ONE-BOWL BATTERS

My favorite baked goods are easy to make and easy to eat. I'm not a fussy baker, nor do I really enjoy complicated desserts. I'm a muffin girl, a pound-cake kinda guy. Once you realize most batters are made of dry ingredients (some kind of flour plus something sweet, like sugar), wet ingredients (often eggs, often fat like oil or butter, sometimes things like canned pumpkin), and something to "season" the batter with flavor (extracts, spices, etc.), you can mix and match as you please to make so many interesting combinations. I also really love to stir something like chocolate chips into batters or top the baked goods with a little something like sliced almonds, as I'm always looking for extra flavor and texture. Keep in mind that all these one-bowl batters can be baked in whatever vessel you want (muffin tin, cake pan, loaf pan, etc.)—other than the shape of the baked good, all that will change is the baking time. For the smallest items (muffins), start checking at around 20 minutes. Start checking heftier items like round and square cakes around 30 minutes and thick loaves around 50 minutes.

ONE-BOWL BATTERS	MAIN DRY INGREDIENTS	LIQUID INGREDIENTS	FLAVOR	STIR IN OR TOP WITH
MORNING GLORY MUFFINS	FLOUR (AP & WW) + SUGAR	EGGS, CRUSHED PINEAPPLE WITH ITS JUICE & OIL	GROUND CINNAMON & GINGER	(STIR IN) CARROTS, PECANS, RAISINS & COCONUT
OLIVE OIL & BUTTERMILK LOAF	FLOUR & SUGAR	EGGS, OLIVE OIL & BUTTERMILK	CITRUS ZEST OR VANILLA OR ANOTHER EXTRACT (OPTIONAL)	(SERVE WITH) WHIPPED CREAM & FRUIT
EASIEST ALMOND CAKE	SUGAR & ALMOND FLOUR	WHOLE EGGS & EGG WHITES	ALMOND EXTRACT	(TOP WITH) SLICED ALMONDS & POWDERED SUGAR
CHOCOLATE ESPRESSO WAKE-UP! CAKE	FLOUR, SUGAR & COCOA POWDER	OIL & ESPRESSO	← FROM COCOA & ESPRESSO	(TOP WITH) CHOCOLATE ICING
PUMPKIN CHOCOLATE CHIP BREAD	FLOUR & BROWN SUGAR	WATER, OIL & CANNED PUMPKIN	PUMPKIN PIE SPICE + CHOCOLATE	(STIR IN) CHOCOLATE CHIPS

MORNING GLORY MUFFINS

I love muffins full of stuff, and Morning Glory muffins—filled with pineapple, carrots, nuts, raisins, and coconut—are one of my absolute favorites. They're basically like carrot cake muffins. They're delicious right out of the oven, but leftovers can be split and put under the broiler or in a toaster oven to crisp them up a bit. Or griddle them in a skillet with butter! There's no wrong way to eat them.

Makes a dozen muffins

1 cup all-purpose flour

1 cup whole wheat flour

½ cup sugar

1 teaspoon baking soda

1 teaspoon baking powder

2 teaspoons ground cinnamon

2 teaspoons ground ginger

½ teaspoon kosher salt

3 large eggs, beaten

One 8-ounce can crushed pineapple in juice

⅔ cup neutral oil (such as vegetable, grapeseed, or canola)

2 carrots, peeled, coarsely grated

½ cup chopped pecans (or any nut)

½ cup golden raisins (or any small pieces of dried fruit)

½ cup shredded coconut (sweetened or not, up to you)

Preheat your oven to 375°F. Line a 12-cup muffin tin with paper liners.

Whisk together the flours, sugar, baking soda, baking powder, spices, and salt in a large bowl. Stir in the eggs, pineapple and its juice, and oil to form a batter. Stir in the carrots, pecans, raisins, and coconut.

Divide the batter evenly among the prepared muffin wells.

Bake the muffins until they're nicely browned and a toothpick inserted in the center of one comes out clean, about 25 minutes. Let the muffins cool before eating.

The muffins can be stored in a tightly covered container at room temperature for up to 3 days or frozen for up to a month.

This is the Olive Oil + Buttermilk Loaf
(the recipe is on the next page). It's the baked
good from this book I make most often!

OLIVE OIL + BUTTERMILK LOAF

I developed this recipe for one of my classes, and it's become a staple in my kitchen. It's a lot like a pound cake, but it has a bit more dimension, with the grassy olive oil and tangy buttermilk; plus, it's faster and easier to make because you don't have to wait for butter to soften, nor do you have to cream butter and sugar together. This batter is also a beautiful canvas for other flavors. Feel free to add citrus zest, poppy seeds, and/or any type of extract you love (it's really sensational with a teaspoon of Fiori di Sicilia, an extract I buy from King Arthur Baking Company that is both vanilla-y and citrusy). It's also wonderful with softly whipped cream and roasted or crushed fruit, or even just a spoonful of jam. Note that the loaf isn't very tall, so don't be alarmed if yours comes out of the pan feeling a little short (short is not bad; my spouse is short, and I love them so much!).

Makes 1 loaf (8 to 10 slices)

Baking spray

1½ cups all-purpose flour

1 cup sugar

½ teaspoon kosher salt

½ teaspoon baking soda

½ teaspoon baking powder

2 large eggs

½ cup extra-virgin olive oil

⅔ cup buttermilk

Preheat your oven to 350°F. Spray a 9-by-5-inch loaf pan with baking spray and line it with a strip of parchment (as in the photo at left, leave enough overhang at each short end so you have "handles").

Place the flour, sugar, salt, baking soda, and baking powder in a medium bowl and whisk well to combine. Add the eggs, olive oil, and buttermilk and whisk until just combined.

Pour the batter into the prepared loaf pan. Bake the cake until it is dark golden brown on top and a toothpick inserted in the center comes out clean, about 50 minutes. Let the cake cool completely before cutting into thick slices and serving.

Leftovers can be stored at room temperature in a container or wrapped in plastic wrap for a few days.

EASIEST ALMOND CAKE

This cake happens to be both dairy-free and gluten-free, so it's a wonderful option for anyone in your life who might want to avoid those ingredients, but it is also my all-time favorite almond cake. It's great for dessert, or served in the afternoon with coffee or tea, or for breakfast. Basically, eat it whenever you want. Since ground almonds have so much fat, this cake stores particularly well and doesn't dry out easily. If you want to riff on the recipe, try any nut flour instead of almond, or add the finely grated zest of an orange or lemon (or both!) for extra flavor.

You will have three egg yolks left over after making this, which I suggest you hold on to for your next egg dish, to make it extra rich, or use them to make homemade aioli or hollandaise, pasta dough, key lime pie, or lemon curd.

Makes one 8-inch cake (about 8 slices)

Baking spray

1 cup sugar

3 large eggs plus 3 large egg whites

½ teaspoon kosher salt

½ teaspoon almond extract

2½ cups almond flour (or finely ground almonds)

A small handful of sliced blanched almonds

Powdered sugar for dusting

Preheat your oven to 350°F. Spray an 8-inch round cake pan with baking spray and line with a circle of parchment.

Place the sugar, whole eggs, egg whites, salt, and almond extract in a large bowl and whisk vigorously for 1 full minute. The mixture will be frothy. Stir in the almond flour until just combined.

Transfer the batter to the prepared pan. Sprinkle the top with the sliced almonds. Bake the cake until the top is golden brown and it feels firm when you press it with your finger, about 35 minutes.

Let the cake cool to room temperature before removing it from the cake pan. Dust the top generously with powdered sugar (use a sieve or a loose-leaf tea steeper), slice into wedges, and serve.

Store leftovers in a covered container at room temperature, or wrap individual slices in plastic and freeze.

CHOCOLATE ESPRESSO WAKE-UP! CAKE

The texture and flavor of this happens-to-be-vegan cake is just like that of a box mix cake, which I mean as the highest compliment. I love coffee, and I find the espresso flavor really complements the chocolate (you can use decaf, if you prefer), but if you're not a coffee person, a cup of chocolate milk, cranberry juice, or orange juice would all be great substitutes in the cake batter (for the icing, a good substitution for the espresso is heavy cream or nondairy creamer). Serve with your favorite coffee or espresso drink to complete the caffeinated picture, or with an ice-cold glass of your favorite type of milk.

Makes one 8-inch square cake (9 squares)

For the cake:
Baking spray

1½ cups all-purpose flour

1 cup sugar

¼ cup unsweetened cocoa powder (natural or Dutch-processed both work)

½ teaspoon kosher salt

1 teaspoon baking soda

⅓ cup neutral oil (such as vegetable, grapeseed, or canola)

1 cup espresso (or strong coffee), at room temperature

For the icing:
1 cup semisweet chocolate chips

2 tablespoons hot espresso (or strong coffee)

2 tablespoons maple syrup

First, make the cake: Preheat your oven to 350°F. Spray an 8-inch square baking pan with baking spray and line with parchment paper.

Place the flour, sugar, cocoa powder, salt, and baking soda in a medium bowl and whisk thoroughly to combine. Add the oil and espresso and stir until well combined (the batter will be quite thin). Pour the batter into the prepared pan.

Bake the cake until a toothpick inserted into the center comes out clean with no batter stuck to it, about 30 minutes. Let the cake cool completely in the pan.

Then make the icing: Place the chocolate chips in a microwave-safe bowl and microwave in 15-second increments, stirring after each, until melted and smooth. Stir in the hot espresso and maple syrup.

To finish, pour the icing over the cake and spread it out with a small offset spatula (or just a spoon) so that it's smooth. Enjoy immediately while the icing is soft, or let it set in the refrigerator for at least 2 hours so that it's firmer (whatever is your preference). Cut into 9 squares and serve!

Leftovers can be stored at room temperature in a container or wrapped in plastic wrap for a few days.

PUMPKIN CHOCOLATE CHIP BREAD

This bread gets all its stability from canned pureed pumpkin, not eggs (making it vegan, just FYI). It's the perfect thing to have on the counter for a quick breakfast on the way to school or work, or as a snack when someone comes home from either of those things (or anything). If you don't have pumpkin pie spice, just use ¾ teaspoon each ground cinnamon and ginger plus ½ teaspoon nutmeg. Note that you will have a little pumpkin puree left over; you can freeze it for future loaves, or add it to just about any soup, stew, or braise. Or mix it into your dog's food!

Makes 1 loaf (8 to 10 slices)

Baking spray

2 cups all-purpose flour

½ teaspoon kosher salt

½ teaspoon baking soda

½ teaspoon baking powder

2 teaspoons pumpkin pie spice (see headnote)

½ cup water

½ cup neutral oil (such as vegetable, grapeseed, or canola)

1 cup canned pumpkin puree

1 cup packed light brown sugar

1 cup dark chocolate chips

Preheat your oven to 350°F. Spray a 9-by-5-inch loaf pan with baking spray and line with a strip of parchment paper (leave enough overhang at each short end so you have "handles," as in the photo on page 268).

Place the flour, salt, baking soda, baking powder, and pumpkin pie spice in a large bowl and whisk well to combine. Using a wooden spoon, stir in the water, oil, pumpkin puree, and brown sugar. Stir in the chocolate chips. The batter will be thick.

Transfer the batter to the prepared pan, spread the top smooth with a spoon or rubber spatula, and bake until a toothpick inserted into the center comes out clean, about 1 hour. Let the bread cool to room temperature before taking it out of the pan, slicing, and serving.

Leftovers can be stored at room temperature in a container or wrapped in plastic wrap for a few days.

FRUITY COBBLERS + CRISPS

A lot like the Savory Pies (page 244), fruity cobblers and crisps consist of two layers: a soft, juicy filling and a drier topping. For the fruit filling, there is, of course, the fruit, plus something to season and thicken the fruit juices (lemon, ginger, cornstarch, etc.). For the topping, there are dry ingredients (flour, oats, ground nuts, etc.) and wet ingredients to turn those into something wonderful when baked (butter, cream, etc.). It's almost like making a roasted jam with a cookie or cake on top.

These are some of my favorite dessert recipes I've ever written, because they're all so forgiving and it's okay if things aren't too precise. All of them would be enhanced by the addition of something creamy (regular or dairy-free) on top—ice cream, whipped cream, yogurt, crème fraîche, sour cream mixed with brown sugar—baker's choice!

FRUITY COBBLERS & CRISPS	FRUIT	SEASONING/ THICKENER	FAT/LIQUID TOPPING INGREDIENTS	MAIN DRY TOPPING INGREDIENTS
PEAR, CHERRY & ALMOND CRISP	SLICED PEARS & FROZEN CHERRIES	SUGAR, LEMON JUICE, ALMOND EXTRACT & CORNSTARCH	BUTTER	SUGAR, ALMOND FLOUR & ROLLED OATS
GINGERY PEACH + BLUEBERRY CAKEY COBBLER	FROZEN PEACHES & FRESH OR FROZEN BLUEBERRIES	SUGAR, LEMON, CORNSTARCH & GROUND GINGER	HEAVY CREAM	FLOUR, CORNMEAL, BAKING POWDER, SALT + SUGAR
APPLE & CRANBERRY CRISP	CRANBERRY SAUCE & SLICED APPLES	LEMON, CORNSTARCH & GROUND CINNAMON	BUTTER	FLOUR, OATS, BROWN SUGAR & CINNAMON
RASPBERRY & CHOCOLATE COBBLER	FROZEN RASPBERRIES	SUGAR, LEMON & CORNSTARCH	EGGS & HEAVY CREAM	FLOUR, SUGAR, COCOA POWDER, BAKING POWDER & SODA & CHOC. CHIPS
PINEAPPLE UPSIDE-DOWN CAKE (A COBBLER, INVERTED)	CANNED PINEAPPLE RINGS & MARASCHINO CHERRIES	DARK BROWN SUGAR & BUTTER	EGGS, SOUR CREAM, VEG OIL & VANILLA	FLOUR, SUGAR, BAKING POWDER/SODA & SALT

PEAR, CHERRY + ALMOND CRISP

I like to make this crisp when I'm entertaining friends who need to avoid gluten, as it just so happens to be gluten-free (you can also make it dairy-free by using vegan butter). You can swap the pears for apples if you'd like, or even do all cherries (just use two packages instead of one). And the cherries can be swapped for any type of berry. This is very easygoing baking, my friends!

Makes 1 crisp (serves about 6)

For the fruit:

3 pears (preferably Bosc), cored, thinly sliced

One 10-ounce package frozen cherries (no need to defrost)

¼ cup sugar

Juice of 1 lemon

½ teaspoon almond extract (or 2 tablespoons amaretto)

2 tablespoons cornstarch

For the topping:

¾ cup sugar

1 cup almond flour (or finely ground almonds)

1 cup rolled oats

½ teaspoon kosher salt

8 tablespoons (1 stick) unsalted butter (regular or vegan), at room temperature

Preheat your oven to 375°F.

First, make the fruit layer: Place the pears, cherries, sugar, lemon juice, almond extract, and cornstarch in a 9-by-13-inch baking dish (or anything similarly sized that can go in the oven) and use your hands to mix everything together.

Next, make the topping: Stir together the sugar, almond flour, oats, and salt in a large bowl. Add the butter and work the mixture with your hands, rubbing it between your fingertips to form large crumbs (some crumbs might remain sandy—that's okay!).

Scatter the topping evenly on the fruit. Bake until the fruit is bubbling and the crumbs are dark golden brown, about 50 minutes.

Allow the crisp to cool for at least 10 minutes, then serve warm or at room temperature.

GINGERY PEACH + BLUEBERRY CAKEY COBBLER

This is a very gingery cobbler, which I love, but if you prefer a bit less zing, you can reduce the amount of ginger and introduce other flavors, like a teaspoon of ground cinnamon and/or a pinch of ground cardamom. I like to use frozen peaches here (peeling peaches is not one of my favorite tasks, and I love the convenience of frozen fruit), but if you have an abundance of fresh summer peaches and don't mind the extra labor, go for it! It's delicious either way.

Makes 1 cobbler (serves about 6 to 8)

For the fruit layer:
One 16-ounce package frozen peaches (no need to defrost)

2 cups fresh or frozen blueberries (no need to defrost if frozen)

¼ cup sugar

2 tablespoons fresh lemon juice

2 tablespoons cornstarch

2 teaspoons ground ginger

Pinch of kosher salt

For the topping:
1 cup all-purpose flour

1 cup yellow cornmeal

1 tablespoon baking powder

¾ cup sugar

Pinch of kosher salt

1½ cups heavy cream

Preheat your oven to 375°F.

First, make the fruit layer: Place the peaches and blueberries in a 9-by-13-inch baking dish (or anything similarly sized that can go in the oven). Add the sugar, lemon juice, cornstarch, ground ginger, and salt. Use your hands to mix everything together.

Next, make the topping: Whisk together the flour, cornmeal, baking powder, sugar, and salt in a large bowl. Stir in the heavy cream.

Spoon the topping evenly over the fruit and spread it into an even layer with the back of your spoon or a small spatula. Bake until the fruit is bubbling and the topping is dark golden brown, about 45 minutes.

Allow the cobbler to cool for at least 10 minutes, then serve warm or at room temperature.

APPLE + CRANBERRY CRISP

My go-to Thanksgiving dessert, this seasonal crisp features a can of cranberry sauce, a bunch of apples, and just the right amount of cinnamon. And it's way easier to make than a pie. Use any type of apples you would for an apple pie (I like Honeycrisp), and feel free to swap in vegan butter, if you'd like (the topping also works beautifully with gluten-free flour if necessary).

Makes 1 crisp (serves about 6 to 8)

For the fruit layer:
One 14-ounce can whole-berry cranberry sauce

3 apples, cored, thinly sliced (no need to peel unless you want to)

2 tablespoons fresh lemon juice

2 tablespoons cornstarch

½ teaspoon ground cinnamon

Pinch of kosher salt

For the topping:
1 cup all-purpose flour

1 cup rolled oats

1 cup packed brown sugar (light or dark)

½ teaspoon kosher salt

1 teaspoon ground cinnamon

12 tablespoons (1½ sticks) unsalted butter, at room temperature

Preheat your oven to 375°F.

First, make the fruit layer: Place all the ingredients in a 9-by-13-inch baking dish (or anything similarly sized that can go in the oven). Mix well with your hands (the cranberry sauce will lose its jellylike texture in the oven!).

Next, make the topping: Stir together the flour, oats, brown sugar, salt, and cinnamon in a large bowl. Add the butter and work the mixture with your hands, rubbing it between your fingertips to form large crumbs. Really scrunch it with your hands, so it's like dense, slightly crumbly cookie dough.

Dot the top of the fruit layer evenly with the crumb mixture. Bake until the fruit is bubbling and the crumbs are dark golden brown, about 45 minutes.

Allow the crisp to cool for at least 10 minutes, then serve warm or at room temperature.

RASPBERRY + CHOCOLATE COBBLER

I love this dessert so much. It's basically like a dense chocolate cake, or a slightly cakey brownie, on top of juicy raspberries. Heaven! It's wonderful with whipped cream. If you buy a pint of cream for the recipe, you'll have an extra cup that you can whip and sweeten with sugar or maple syrup, if you'd like. Or just serve with a can of whipped cream! And/or ice cream!

Makes 1 cobbler (serves about 6)

For the raspberries:
One 10-ounce package frozen raspberries (no need to defrost)

¼ cup sugar

Juice of half a lemon

1 tablespoon cornstarch

Pinch of kosher salt

For the topping:
1 cup all-purpose flour

½ cup sugar, plus a tablespoon for sprinkling

⅓ cup unsweetened cocoa powder (natural or Dutch-processed both work)

½ teaspoon baking powder

½ teaspoon baking soda

Pinch of kosher salt

2 large eggs

1 cup heavy cream

1 cup semisweet chocolate chips

Preheat your oven to 375°F.

First, prepare the raspberry layer: Place the raspberries in a 9-inch pie dish (or anything similarly sized that can go in the oven). Add the sugar, lemon juice, cornstarch, and salt and mix well.

Next, make the topping: Whisk together the flour, sugar, cocoa powder, baking powder, baking soda, and salt in a large bowl. Add the eggs and heavy cream and stir well to combine. Stir in the chocolate chips. The batter will be thick.

Spread the topping evenly over the raspberries. Sprinkle the tablespoon of sugar evenly on top.

Bake just until the topping is set (it should be firm to the touch), the raspberries are bubbling, and your kitchen smells wonderfully chocolatey, 50 minutes.

Allow the cobbler to cool for at least 10 minutes, then serve warm or at room temperature.

PINEAPPLE UPSIDE-DOWN CAKE (A COBBLER, INVERTED)

I love an upside-down cake, and this recipe is such a crowd-pleaser. It's beautiful in a fun retro way, and I dare you to find a more delicious use of canned fruit. The cake part of the recipe is a fantastic yellow cake, and if you ever want to just make the cake without the pineapple part, note that the batter requires ¾ cup pineapple juice (not listed in the ingredients below because it comes from the can of pineapple rings; you could also substitute orange juice).

Makes 1 cake (serves about 10)

For the pineapple part:
4 tablespoons (½ stick) unsalted butter

½ cup packed brown sugar (light or dark)

One 20-ounce can pineapple rings in juice

10 maraschino cherries or frozen cherries

For the cake part:
2 large eggs

½ cup sour cream

½ cup neutral oil (such as vegetable, grapeseed, or canola)

2 teaspoons vanilla extract

2 teaspoons baking powder

1 teaspoon baking soda

½ teaspoon kosher salt

1 cup sugar

2 cups all-purpose flour

Preheat your oven to 350°F.

First, make the pineapple part: Place the butter in an 11-inch cast-iron skillet or a 9-by-13-inch baking dish and place it in the oven until the butter melts. Remove it from the oven and use a pastry brush or rubber spatula to spread the butter so that it coats the bottom and sides of the skillet/dish. Sprinkle the brown sugar evenly over the bottom.

Pour the contents of the pineapple can into a large bowl. Place the pineapple rings (RESERVE THE JUICE!) in a single layer on top of the butter/sugar mixture (break up rings into smaller pieces as needed so that the pineapple stays in a single layer and doesn't overlap). Place a cherry in the center of each whole pineapple ring.

Next, make the cake part: Add the eggs to the reserved pineapple juice along with the sour cream, oil, and vanilla, and whisk well to combine. Add the baking powder, baking soda, salt, and sugar and whisk really vigorously to make sure everything is evenly incorporated (the mixture might become a bit foamy, which is just the leavening mixing with the acidic pineapple juice: cool!). Whisk in the flour until just combined.

Pour the batter evenly over the pineapple slices. Bake the cake until it's dark golden brown and a toothpick inserted in the center comes out clean, about 35 minutes.

Let the cake cool for at least 20 minutes. Invert the cake (see next page), cut into pieces, and serve warm or at room temperature.

To invert the cake, run a dinner knife around the edge of the skillet or baking dish to loosen the cake from the sides. Put a serving platter or cutting board on top of the skillet or dish and carefully but assertively turn the whole thing over to invert the cake onto the platter. If any of the brown sugar mixture and/or pineapples stick to the pan, simply use a knife or a spoon to dislodge it/them and put them back on top of the cake. No biggie!

A CONVERSATION WITH MY COUSIN IVY + MY MOM ABOUT THE BAKERY

If you've ever heard me talk about my work (or just my life), I've probably told you that my maternal grandparents ran a bakery in Brooklyn. It was called Ratchick's, which was their last name, and was on Avenue J and East 15th Street in Midwood, directly across the street from the famed Di Fara pizzeria.

My family's baking roots go back generations. My grandfather Julius (who I am named after) was born in Belarus, the son of a flour miller. My grandmother Beatrice was born in Ukraine, the daughter of a baker. During the pogroms, her family fled to Belarus, where she met and married my grandfather. Together they sought refuge in America. Most of their family members did not make it out of Eastern Europe.

Their journey took them first through France, and then through Cuba, where my grandmother stayed for a year while my grandfather went ahead to Duryea, Pennsylvania, to find distant relatives. After my grandmother joined my grandfather in Pennsylvania, they had two daughters, my aunts Debby and Renee. They eventually relocated to the Bronx, where my mother was born, and then to Brooklyn, where they spent the rest of their lives running the bakery.

I was born after both my grandparents had died and the bakery was out of my family's hands (it turned into a kosher bakery called Isaac's Bake Shop, which sadly burned down in 2022). Though I never knew my grandparents or experienced being in the bakery when my family ran it (my mom, aunts, and cousins worked there), I carry them all with me. I feel their presence the most when I'm in my kitchen and when I talk to my family about them. I thought it would be meaningful to share a conversation between me; my mother, Rochelle; and my cousin Ivy (Aunt Debby's daughter) in

this book. Sharing about my family feels like one of the best ways to honor the privilege of publishing books. They get to live on in these pages, and in you knowing more about them. Thank you for helping to carry their torch.

Julia: What are your earliest memories of the bakery?

Ivy: Walking to the bakery from the house I grew up in. I remember that was always very exciting to me because the whole family was there. I remember being very excited about when I would be old enough to work there.

Julia: When were you old enough to work there?

Ivy: When I was a little girl, they would let me fold boxes. They'd give me a quarter for, like, every hundred boxes I would fold. Just to crack the corners. And then I probably started working there when I was about fourteen. With my brother and my cousins. That was the best part of it, just being there together. It was the hub of our family. And I miss that a lot. We became this staple in the neighborhood and all my friends would come in with their parents. Especially around the holidays. It was that cool family, neighborhood-y, community feeling.

Julia: Mom, what are your earliest memories?

Rochelle: Eating buttercream out of the vat in the back! I also had the same apprenticeship that Ivy had. My introduction was cracking the boxes and making them halfway. So you could slip a cake in. And I would get pennies. Not quarters.

Ivy: Quarters for every hundred! Every hundred!

Julia: I feel like I've always heard just about everything behind the counter and the family. Do either of you have any particular memories of customers? Were there any, like, regulars that stand out?

Ivy: For me, it was definitely friends' parents. I would be like, "Oh, Lonnie's father came in today." I would go and tell somebody else, you know? I do remember people pointing out particular things. "I want that rye bread." I'd point to the one I thought they wanted and they'd be like, "No, no, that one behind it." I remember that driving me nuts.

Rochelle: And if they wanted half a rye, they wanted to make sure they got the bigger half. I remember taking the halves and holding them to show them they were equal. Do you remember that, Ivy?

Ivy: Yep! And everything was with or without. With or without cheese. With or without raisins. With or without whatever. I remember rolls would drive you nuts, because there were like a hundred of them in there. "I wanna see the roll. Can you turn it?" I remember losing my shit with that.

Rochelle: Especially the people who wanted things well-done. The well-done people wanted it really baked out dark.

Julia: Mom, you're a well-done person!

Rochelle: I am. I am a well-done person.

Ivy: People were picky. I didn't have a lot of patience for that. And my mother certainly had no patience for that.

Rochelle: She had no patience for anything.

Julia: Ivy, it sounds like you were so excited to be associated with the bakery. Mom, when you were growing up, was it something you were proud of?

Rochelle: I was, I was. I was very proud of being related to the bakery—until I wasn't. I'd say probably my junior year in high school is when that began. I felt diminished by it, because everyone in my class was so competitive about going to college and doing something other than working in a bakery. I was caught between an aspirational idea and what felt like a betrayal of my background. I started to drift away. School became very, very important. Socializing became very, very important. I didn't socialize in the bakery the way Ivy did.

Julia: When did it become something that you became sort of reattached to?

Rochelle: Probably in my late twenties. I had this moment where I felt like I missed it. I really missed it. I missed stacking the trays. I loved decorating the window. I loved coming in and laying cookies out and making the cookies with the chocolate leaves on top.

Ivy: Aunt Rochelle, do you remember when we got held up?

Rochelle: Yes! When was it?

Ivy: It was Christmas Day 1976. I remember the year because I was sixteen. It was my mother, my cousin Alan, and me. It was Christmas night and a guy walked in and held us up at gunpoint. We were all behind the counter. I was speechless. The guy says to give him all of our cash. Alan opened the register, looked up, and asked, "Box or bag?"

Julia: That's amazing.

Ivy: That story will stick with me forever.

Julia: Okay, without overthinking it, and I'll give you both a second to think about it before you answer so you don't influence each other, what was your favorite thing to eat from the bakery?

Ivy: I would say mine was probably the seven-layer cake.

Julia: Mom?

Rochelle: I would say the heels of the bread. I actually love the taste of the crust, but part of it was being sneaky. Because it was forbidden to sneak the heels of the bread. So then I would feel guilty about it, which is sort of my natural state of being.

Julia: Feeling guilty is your natural state of being?

Rochelle: Yes, I think so. You know something I just remembered? When I was in first or second grade, for my birthday, I brought cupcakes to my class with everybody's names on them. This was a big, big deal. I mean, I have to tell you, when those cupcakes came and everybody had their name, I felt so proud.

Julia: When you walk into a bakery today, not necessarily like a Jewish bakery, but just like any bakery, how do you feel when you open the door?

Ivy: The one thing that hits me every time, every freaking time, is I want to tie boxes.

Rochelle: I feel like I want to inspect everything. I'm so like my father, I turn the bread over to see how it's baked. I look for the holes in the bread. I look for the quality of the crust. I look at the bottom of every loaf, because my father would turn everything over to see how it was baked. He could tell who baked that morning just by looking at the bread.

Ivy: Oh, I just remembered something else I loved that you can't find anywhere. Chocolate-covered jelly doughnuts. Mmmmm.

Rochelle: I remember those.

Julia: What lessons do you both carry with you from the bakery? Are there things in your day-to-day lives now that you learned from the bakery?

Rochelle: Absolutely. It's all about the customer. It's all about who you're talking to. I loved our customers because, first of all, they provided a roof over my head. I actually liked it when they specified what they wanted, because it was important to them to get something particular, and we could fulfill that promise. Over time, it became very clear to me how important this bakery was in the neighborhood, especially at holiday times. Lines would go around the block and people would wait to buy things. So for me, the best lesson was to listen to customers, or listen to my students, or listen to my family the best I could. To really try to understand what it is that they're feeling. To really understand what they're really asking for.

Ivy: I miss it terribly, actually. I really miss it.

Julia: That was going to be my last question. What do you miss about the bakery?

Ivy: I miss being with my family. You know, we were together all the time.

Julia: What do you miss, Mom? When you write about your memories about the bakery and create artwork about it, what are you trying to get at?

Rochelle: To identify myself. I do it, and I feel more complete.

Ivy: I get that. I get it. I understand.

Julia: I do too. I feel like that's what I try to do in a way with every recipe.

Rochelle: It's like there's something buried and you just want to uncover it.

Ivy: And you don't appreciate it clearly until you're older. It's huge. I mean, the bakery is huge. And it's a huge part of my identity.

Julia: I feel like it's a huge part of my identity, and I was never even there.

Rochelle: It looms over all of us. I think of people who grow up in homes that don't have much of a direction in one way or another. The bakery gave us so much purpose.

Julia: It's such an anchor. I always love hearing about it, and it's nice to hear about it from the two of you together.

MENU SUGGESTIONS

Planning a menu is a great lesson in figuring out, quite literally, what goes with what. To help demonstrate how I approach menu-planning, I've prepared this chart for you. In addition, when you turn the page you'll find a BUNCH of menus that answer the needs of specific scenarios. Even if you're not making a big meal with lots of parts, I hope it's helpful to see how I put things together.

THEME	MAIN PROTEIN (NOT NECESSARILY MEAT)
PASTA NIGHT	MEATBALLS!
SOUP + SALAD	A POT OF GREAT SOUP
HOLIDAY MEAL	ROAST TURKEY, A WHOLE FISH OR STUFFED SQUASH
A PICNIC	SANDWICHES
BRUNCH	A FRITTATA

SALAD OR VEG	CARBY THING	OPTIONAL EXTRA THING	DESSERT
CAESAR SALAD	SPAGHETTI	GARLIC BREAD	STORE-BOUGHT CANNOLI
A FUN CHOPPED SALAD	WARM BREAD	A BIG WEDGE OF CHEESE	BROWNIES
SIMPLY DRESSED CHICORIES	MASHED POTATOES	ROASTED BRUSSELS SPROUTS	PIE & ICE CREAM
CUT-UP VEGGIES	CHIPS	DIP	COOKIES
FRUIT SALAD	HASH BROWNS	BACON	PASTRIES (PURCHASE!)

Planning menus is probably my favorite pastime (!), but when people ask me how I do it, I always struggle to find a satisfying answer. "You just put the things together!" I think to myself, not realizing this process isn't as intuitive for everyone as it is for me. Thinking about this also makes me understand, in turn, how other endeavors that seem inscrutable to me (composing music, choreographing a dance) are actually intuitive for some. It's amazing how we are all so diverse in our thinking.

I hope the chart on the previous page unlocks something for you, and the menus that follow give you plenty of ideas for figuring out how to match a menu to a moment. As with everything in cooking, I think the most important things to keep in mind with menu planning are to lean into abundance over scarcity and flexibility over rigidity.

While these menus predominantly feature recipes from this very book, note that the items in italics are not recipes in the book, just suggestions for things that would work well in the menu. Most of these suggestions are for things that don't have to be cooked, just purchased (store-bought cookies and ice cream for dessert, for example). Remember that not every part of every meal has to be made from scratch. You certainly don't need my permission to buy or delegate something rather than cook it, but if it's helpful to hear someone say it, then please allow me to offer you the option to take it easy on yourself, especially in the kitchen!

I'm Hosting Book Club for Ten People
Kinda Sicilian Spaghetti (× 2)
Roasted Brussels Sprouts with Sherry
   Vinaigrette + Manchego (× 2)
Easiest Almond Cake
Softly Whipped Cream

It's Our Anniversary and I Want to Make Something Special Just for Us
Chicken Francese
Favorite Broccoli Rabe
Raspberry + Chocolate Cobbler

A Couple of Friends Are Coming Over at the Last Minute
Grandma's Raw Tomato Ziti
Italian Chopped Salad
Ice Cream + Store-Bought Cookies

It's Passover and There Are Eight Vegetarians
Tomato, White Bean + Fennel Stew (× 2)
Chickpea + Spinach Rice (× 2)
A Great Carrot Salad (× 2)
Peppery Zucchini with Whipped Feta (× 2)

Friends with Little Kids Are Coming Over
Fastest Chicken Noodle Soup
BLTs
Olive Oil + Buttermilk Loaf

I'm Hosting a Fall/Winter Holiday Dinner for Eight People
Braised Pork with Apricots + Green Olives (×2)
Some Great Bread
Spiced Chickpea Squash Bowls (× 2)
Shaved Fennel + Apple Salad (× 2)
Apple + Cranberry Crisp
Store-Bought Pumpkin Pie
Vanilla Ice Cream

What to Serve with a Pitcher of Margaritas
Chicken Fajitas with Poblanos + Onions
Roasted Sweet Potatoes with Salsa Macha
Warm Flour Tortillas
Lime Wedges, Hot Sauce, Sour Cream, Grated
   Cheese, Shredded Lettuce, and/or Guacamole

I'm Going On a Daylong Road Trip
Morning Glory Muffins
Best Ham Sandwich
Tahini Ranch Dressing *and a Bunch of Vegetables*

**My Friends Just Had a Baby and
I Want to Stock Their Freezer**
Creamy Tomato + Coconut Soup
Mushroom Cacciatore
Italian Sausage + Ricotta Meatballs
Black Bean + Cheddar Cornbread Pie

**My Neighbor Just Had Surgery and
Could Use a Helping Hand**
Farro + Roasted Vegetable Salad
Turkey + Green Chile Chili
Jennie's Curried Chicken + Potatoes
Pumpkin Chocolate Chip Bread

**My Extended Family Is Coming Over,
and There Are So Many Dietary Restrictions**
Vegan Kale Caesar with Crispy Chickpeas
Beef, Spinach + Feta Meatballs
Lentil + Sweet Potato Shepherd's Pie
Roasted Squash Agrodolce
Pear, Cherry + Almond Crisp
   (made with vegan butter)

**We Were Invited to a Barbecue and
Asked to Bring Something**
Best Tuna Mac Salad
Pineapple Upside-Down Cake
   (A Cobbler, Inverted)

**I Work From Home and Want to
Make Myself a Grown-Up Lunch**
Shrimp + Grits Bowl
A Glass of Nice Wine

Summer Dinner Outside
Everything-Bagel Salmon + Smashed Potatoes
Skillet Succotash
Gingery Peach + Blueberry Cakey Cobbler

Cozy Cold-Weather Dinner
Classic Caesar with Big Crunchy Croutons
Chicken Scarpariello
Spaghetti with Olive Oil, Garlic + Parmesan
Chocolate Espresso Wake-Up! Cake

**Dinner with Friends in a
Summertime Rental House**
Caesar Spaghetti
Braised Eggplant with Tomatoes + Golden Raisins
A Platter of Sliced Cucumbers, Tomatoes +
   Mozzarella with Pizzeria Vinaigrette
Watermelon Wedges + Cherries

Deceptively Fast Weeknight Dinner
Spicy Chicken with Lime + Cashews
Gingery Baby Bok Choy
Hot Buttery Rice

Another Deceptively Fast Weeknight Dinner
Frozen-Fish Chowder
Bibb Lettuce + Cherry Tomato Salad with
   Creamy Mustard Dressing
Hot Kaiser Rolls + Cold Butter

**Why Not One More Deceptively
Fast Weeknight Dinner?**
Chicken + Kimchi Rice
Cucumber + Avocado Salad

CONVERSION TABLE

LIQUIDS

¼ cup = 60 ml

⅓ cup = 80 ml

½ cup = 120 ml

⅔ cup = 160 ml

¾ cup = 180 ml

1 cup = 240 ml

2 cups = 480 ml

MAYONNAISE AND YOGURT

1 cup = 220 g

BUTTER

1 tablespoon = 14 g

2 tablespoons = 28 g

4 tablespoons = ½ stick = 56 g

8 tablespoons = 1 stick = 113 g

ALL-PURPOSE FLOUR AND WHOLE WHEAT FLOUR

1 cup = 125 g

GRANULATED SUGAR

1 cup = 200 g

LONG-GRAIN WHITE RICE

1 cup = 200 g

KOSHER SALT
(I use Diamond Crystal)

1 teaspoon = 4 g

OVEN TEMPERATURES

300°F = 150°C

350°F = 175°C

375°F = 190°C

400°F = 200°C

425°F = 220°C

WEIGHTS

¼ pound = 113 g

½ pound = 227 g

¾ pound = 340 g

1 pound = 455 g

MEASUREMENTS

1 inch = 2½ cm

2 inches = 5 cm

3 inches = 7½ cm

4 inches = 10 cm

5 inches = 12½ cm

6 inches = 15 cm

7 inches = 17½ cm

8 inches = 20 cm

9 inches = 22½ cm

10 inches = 25 cm

11 inches = 27½ cm

12 inches = 30 cm

Here I am acting totally casual (!!) leaning against a garage door at Treadlight Farm, the incredible flower farm that neighbors Long Season Farm.

THANK YOU TO . . .

My parents for designing this book. What a joy!! Mom, thank you for also coming up with the title, for showing up for all my classes, and for taking the most beautiful notes. Your attention is such a buoy. Thank you for showing me the value of a chart (!) and for always thinking outside the box, so I can see what that looks like. Dad, thank you for your attention to detail and your love of beautiful things, for cooking along in my classes, and for never letting me drink alone. Thank you for caring so much about all the little design things and not losing sight of the big picture.

Steve Turner for all your hard work (and I'm sorry we never made my handwriting a font). And Steve Walkowiak for your help with so much scanning.

Julie Will for saying yes and taking me with you. And Megan Lynch and the whole Flatiron Books group for welcoming me. Thanks to Kate Lucas for their support. And thank you to Judith Sutton for being the most consistent and thorough copy editor.

Haley Scarpino for testing all these recipes and offering invaluable notes, and for being such an incredible support and asset in all my classes. I feel so lucky you're in my corner!

Natalie Chitwood for such a glorious day of photography (and Margo Sivin for the photo of the Gay Soiréeeee, Erin Enouen for the photo of me and the Brussels sprouts, and Chris Bonney for giving Grace the camera that I borrowed for a year to take all the rest of the photos).

Every single person who has ever taken one of my classes (including my grandma, who thinks I am on television every weekend). Thank you

for showing up and for supporting my work. You remind me why I love this work, and you have deepened my love for it.

Every single person who opens my newsletter every week. Your support means so much.

All the librarians, teachers, bookstore owners, and people who work in bookstores. Thank you for believing in, protecting, and celebrating books and the communities that form around them. You make our world so much safer and better.

My coach, Matt, for all the liftoffs, literal and figurative, and the Sunday morning Queer Barbell Club for being such a fun, supportive community.

Cassandra, our therapist, for helping us so much. Carmen, especially for "of course."

Emmet, Stephen, and Timmy for making Full Fridge Club something I look forward to every Monday.

The entire Long Season Farm crew for growing the best vegetables and for being great neighbors. Thanks for always including me.

My friends who make my life full of so much love, connection, and fun. To the Card Night crew for being my family, including the Brock/Talbot family, who make me feel like the luckiest uncle around.

Ben, Kait, Remy, Louis, Ivy, Jennie, Urban, and the rest of my family for the love and support.

Grace, Hope, Winky, Leo, and Papaguy for being my whole heart, my home, the simmering pot that's always on the stove.

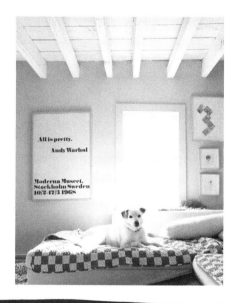

INDEX

acorn squash, 104

Agrodolce, Roasted Squash, *83, 84, 85*

air fryers, 161

almond flour/almond extract

Easiest Almond Cake, *263, 270, 271*

Pear, Cherry + Almond Crisp, *277, 278, 279*

almonds

Easiest Almond Cake, *263, 270, 271*

A Great Carrot Salad, *41, 50, 51*

My Usual Chopped Salad, *29, 38, 39*

anchovy fillets

Caesar Spaghetti, *189,* 190, *191*

Classic Caesar with Big Crunchy Croutons, *29,* 30, *31*

Any-Bean Soup, *113,* 120, *121*

apples

Apple + Cranberry Crisp, *277, 282, 283*

Shaved Fennel + Apple Salad, *41, 46, 47*

Apricots + Green Olives, Braised Pork with, *149, 158, 159*

artichoke hearts

Chicken with Artichokes, Sun-Dried Tomatoes + Feta, *221, 222, 223*

Italian Chopped Salad, *29, 34, 35*

avocados, 42

Baby Bok Choy, Gingery, *71, 80, 81*

bacon

BLT, *54–55,* 56, 57

Roasted Broccoli + Peanut Salad, *41, 52, 53*

Shrimp + Bacon Rice, *165, 174, 175*

Shrimp + Grits Bowl, *176–77, 184, 185*

Tomatoes Casino, *95,* 102, *103*

baked goods. *See* fruity cobblers and crisps; one-bowl batters; savory pies

barbecue sauce, 240

basil

Grandma's Raw Tomato Ziti, *189, 196, 197*

Roasted Fish + Cauliflower with Sicilian Tomato Salad, *233, 238, 239*

bay leaves, 158

BBQ Tofu + Sweet Potato Fries, *233, 240, 241*

beans, canned

Black Bean + Cheddar Cornbread Pie, *245, 252, 253*

Minestrone-ish, *113,* 118, *119*

Tomato, White Bean + Fennel Stew, *137, 146, 147*

Turkey + Green Chile Chili, *137, 144, 145*

White Bean, Roasted Tomato + Polenta Pie, *245, 248, 249*

beans, dried, *122*

Any-Bean Soup, *113,* 120, *121*

cooking and measuring tips, *123*

beef, ground

Beef, Spinach + Feta Meatballs, *209,* 214, *215*

Italian Wedding Soup, *113, 116, 117*

Mushroom Swiss Burger Rice, *165, 172,* 173

bell peppers

Biscuits + Gravy Pie, *245, 254, 255*

Black Bean + Cheddar Cornbread Pie, *245, 252, 253*

Chicken Fajitas with Poblanos + Onions, *221,* 230, 231

Chicken Scarpariello, *149, 156,* 157

Chorizo + Sofrito Rice, *165, 166, 167*

Feta + Rice-Stuffed Peppers, *95, 96, 97*

Mushroom Cacciatore, *137, 138, 139*

Best Ham Sandwich, *54–55,* 62, *63*

Best Tuna Mac Salad, *189,* 198, *199*

Better Than Bouillon, 160

Fastest Chicken Noodle Soup, *113,* 114, 115

Bibimbap (Aka the Original Grain Bowl), *176–177,* 178, *179*

Biscuits + Gravy Pie, *245,* 254, *255*

blenders, 160

BLT, *54–55,* 56, 57

Blueberry Cakey Cobbler, Gingery Peach +, *277,* 280, *281*

body image conversation, 202–5

braises

basic formula, 148, *149*

Braised Eggplant with
    Tomatoes + Golden Raisins,
    149, 150, *151*
Braised Fish with Cream +
    Dill, *149*, 154, *155*
Braised Pork with Apricots +
    Green Olives, *149*, 158, *159*
Braised Spiced Lamb
    Meatballs, *209*, 210, *211*
Chicken Scarpariello, *149*,
    156, *157*
Soy-Braised Tofu with
    Scallions, *149*, 152, *153*
broccoli
    Roasted Broccoli + Peanut
        Salad, *41*, 52, *53*
    Roasted Broccoli with Carrot-
        Miso Dressing, *83*, 88, *89*
    Sticky Pork with Broccoli,
        233, 242, *243*
    Stir-Fried Hoisin Chicken +
        Broccoli, *221*, 226, *227*
Broccoli Rabe, Favorite, *71*, 72,
    73
brothy soups
    Any-Bean Soup, *113*, 120, *121*
    basic formula, 112, *113*
    Fastest Chicken Noodle
        Soup, *113*, 114, *115*
    Frozen-Fish Chowder, *113*,
        124, 125
    Italian Wedding Soup, *113*,
        116, *117*
    Minestrone-ish, *113*, 118, *119*
Brussels sprouts
    Rice + Lentil Bowl with All the
        Toppings, *176–177*, *182*, 183
    Roasted Brussels Sprouts
        with Sherry Vinaigrette +
        Manchego, *83*, 86, *87*
butter lettuce, 59
buttermilk
    Black Bean + Cheddar
        Cornbread Pie, *245*, 252,
        253

Olive Oil + Buttermilk Loaf,
    263, 266–267, 269
Peppery Zucchini with
    Whipped Feta, *71*, 78, *79*
buttermilk biscuits, 254
butternut squash
    Roasted Squash Soup, *127*,
        129, 130, *131*
    Winter Chopped Salad, *29*,
        36, 37

cabbage
    Minestrone-ish, *113*, 118, *119*
    My Usual Chopped Salad, *29*,
        38, *39*
    Winter Chopped Salad, *29*,
        36, 37
Cacciatore, Mushroom, *137*, 138,
    139
Cacio e Pepe Potatoes, Twice-
    Baked, *95*, 98, 99
Caesar Spaghetti, *189*, 190, *191*
Caesar with Big Crunchy
    Croutons, Classic, *29*, 30, *31*
Caesar with Crispy Chickpeas,
    Vegan Kale, *29*, 32, *33*
cakes
    Chocolate Espresso Wake-
        Up! Cake, *263*, 272, *273*
    Easiest Almond Cake, *263*,
        270, *271*
    Pineapple Upside-Down Cake
        (A Cobbler, Inverted), *277*,
        286, 287, *288–89*
capers
    Best Tuna Mac Salad, *189*,
        198, *199*
    Braised Eggplant with
        Tomatoes + Golden Raisins,
        149, 150, *151*
    Kinda Sicilian Spaghetti, *189*,
        200, *201*
    Vegan Kale Caesar with
        Crispy Chickpeas, *29*, 32, *33*

carrots
    Any-Bean Soup, *113*, 120, *121*
    Bibimbap (Aka the Original
        Grain Bowl), *176–77*, 178,
        179
    Carrot Ginger Soup, *127*, *129*,
        132
    Carrots with Coriander +
        Cilantro, *71*, 76, *77*
    Fastest Chicken Noodle
        Soup, *113*, 114, *115*
    A Great Carrot Salad, *41*,
        50, *51*
    Jennie's Curried Chicken +
        Potatoes, *137*, 140, *141*
    Minestrone-ish, *113*, 118, *119*
    Morning Glory Muffins, *263*,
        264, 265
    My Favorite Veggie Sandwich,
        54–55, 58, 59, *60–61*
    My Usual Chopped Salad, *29*,
        38, *39*
    Roasted Broccoli with Carrot-
        Miso Dressing, *83*, 88, *89*
Cashews, Spicy Chicken with
    Lime +, *221*, 228, *229*
Cauliflower with Sicilian Tomato
    Salad, Roasted Fish +, *233*,
    238, 239
cayenne pepper
    Chorizo + Sofrito Rice, *165*,
        166, *167*
    Spicy Sweet Potato Soup, *127*,
        128–29, *133*, 135
celery
    Best Tuna Mac Salad, *189*,
        198, *199*
    Frozen-Fish Chowder, *113*,
        124, *125*
    A Great Tuna Sandwich,
        54–55, 56, 59, *60–61*
    Roasted Fish + Cauliflower
        with Sicilian Tomato Salad,
        233, *238*, 239

cheddar cheese
Best Ham Sandwich, *54–55,*
62, 63
Black Bean + Cheddar
Cornbread Pie, *245, 252,*
253
My Favorite Veggie Sandwich,
54–55, 58, 59, 60–61
cheese. *See specific cheeses*
cherries
Pear, Cherry + Almond Crisp,
277, 278, 279
Pineapple Upside-Down Cake
(A Cobbler, Inverted), *277,*
286, 287, 288–89
chicken, ground, 216
chicken, rotisserie, 246
chicken breasts
Chicken Fajitas with Poblanos
+ Onions, *221, 230, 231*
Chicken Francese, *221, 224,*
225
Chicken + Kimchi Rice, *165,*
170, 171
Chicken Scarpariello, *149,*
156, 157
Chicken with Artichokes,
Sun-Dried Tomatoes + Feta,
221, 222, 223
Cold Roast Chicken
Sandwich, *54–55, 58, 59,*
60–61
Fastest Chicken Noodle
Soup, *113, 114,* 115
Spicy Chicken with Lime +
Cashews, *221, 228, 229*
Stir-Fried Hoisin Chicken +
Broccoli, *221, 226, 227*
chicken thighs
Chicken + Kimchi Rice, *165,*
170, 171
Jennie's Curried Chicken +
Potatoes, *137, 140,* 141

chickpeas
Chickpea + Spinach Rice, *165,*
168, 169
Farmers' Lunch Pasta, *189,*
192, 193
My Usual Chopped Salad, *29,*
38, 39
Spiced Chickpea Squash
Bowls, *95, 104, 105*
Vegan Kale Caesar with
Crispy Chickpeas, *29, 32, 33*
Child of the '90s Bowl, *176–77,*
186, 187
chiles
Roasted Sweet Potatoes with
Salsa Macha, *83, 90, 91*
Turkey + Green Chile Chili,
137, 144, 145
chives
Frozen-Fish Chowder, *113,*
124, 125
Skillet Succotash, *71, 74, 75*
Tahini Ranch Dressing, *23,*
25, 27
chocolate chips
Chocolate Espresso Wake-
Up! Cake, *263, 272, 273*
Pumpkin Chocolate Chip
Bread, *263, 274, 275*
Raspberry + Chocolate
Cobbler, *277, 284, 285*
chopped salads
Italian Chopped Salad, *29,*
34, 35
My Usual Chopped Salad, *29,*
38, 39
Winter Chopped Salad, *29,*
36, 37
Chorizo + Sofrito Rice, *165,* 166,
167
Chowder, Frozen-Fish, *113, 124,*
125
cilantro
Carrots with Coriander +
Cilantro, *71, 76, 77*

Spiced Chickpea Squash
Bowls, *95, 104, 105*
cinnamon
Apple + Cranberry Crisp, *277,*
282, 283
Morning Glory Muffins, *263,*
264, 265
Spiced Chickpea Squash
Bowls, *95, 104, 105*
Classic Caesar with Big Crunchy
Croutons, *29, 30, 31*
cobblers. *See fruity cobblers and*
crisps
cocoa powder
Chocolate Espresso Wake-
Up! Cake, *263, 272, 273*
Raspberry + Chocolate
Cobbler, *277, 284, 285*
coconut, 265
coconut flakes, 134
coconut milk
Carrot Ginger Soup, *127, 129,*
132
Creamy Tomato + Coconut
Soup, *127, 128, 133, 134,* 134
Lentil + Sweet Potato
Shepherd's Pie, *245, 250,*
251
Red Curry Corn Soup, *127,*
128, 133, 133
Roasted Squash Soup, *127,*
129, 130, 131
Vegetable + Tofu Coconut
Curry, *137, 142, 143*
cod fillets
Braised Fish with Cream +
Dill, *149, 154, 155*
Frozen-Fish Chowder, *113,*
124, 125
Roasted Fish + Cauliflower
with Sicilian Tomato Salad,
233, 238, 239
Cold Roast Chicken Sandwich,
54–55, 58, 59, 60–61
collard greens, 184

conversion table, 299
cooking philosophy, 10–11
coriander
    Braised Spiced Lamb
      Meatballs, *209, 210, 211*
    Carrots with Coriander +
      Cilantro, *71, 76, 77*
    Chickpea + Spinach Rice, *165,*
      168, 169
    Lentil + Sweet Potato
      Shepherd's Pie, *245, 250,*
      251
    Rice + Lentil Bowl with All the
      Toppings, *176–177, 182,* 183
    Roasted Squash Soup, *127,*
      129, 130, *131*
    Spiced Chickpea Squash
      Bowls, *95,* 104, *105*
corn
    Frozen-Fish Chowder, *113,*
      124, 125
    Red Curry Corn Soup, *127,*
      128, 133, *133*
    Skillet Succotash, *71, 74, 75*
cornmeal
    Black Bean + Cheddar
      Cornbread Pie, *245, 252,*
      253
    Gingery Peach + Blueberry
      Cakey Cobbler, *277, 280,*
      281
cranberries, 186
cranberry sauce, 283
cream, heavy
    Braised Fish with Cream +
      Dill, *149, 154, 155*
    Frozen-Fish Chowder, *113,*
      124, 125
    Gingery Peach + Blueberry
      Cakey Cobbler, *277, 280,*
      281
    Raspberry + Chocolate
      Cobbler, *277, 284, 285*
    Roasted Chicken Pot Pie,
      245, 246, 247

Creamy Lemon Dressing, *23,*
  24, 25
Creamy Mustard Dressing, *23,*
  25, 26
Creamy Tomato + Coconut
  Soup, *127, 128, 133,* 134, *134*
crisps. *See* fruity cobblers and
  crisps
croutons, 30
cucumbers
    Cucumber + Avocado Salad,
      41, 42, 43
    Greek Orzo Bowl, *176–77,*
      180, *181*
    My Favorite Veggie Sandwich,
      54–55, 58, 59, 60–61
cumin
    Black Bean + Cheddar
      Cornbread Pie, *245, 252,*
      253
    Braised Spiced Lamb
      Meatballs, *209, 210, 211*
    Chicken Fajitas with Poblanos
      + Onions, *221, 230,* 231
    Chorizo + Sofrito Rice, *165,*
      166, *167*
    Rice + Lentil Bowl with All the
      Toppings, *176–177, 182,* 183
    Spiced Chickpea Squash
      Bowls, *95,* 104, *105*
    Turkey + Green Chile Chili,
      137, 144, *145*
curry paste
    Red Curry Corn Soup, *127,*
      128, 133, *133*
    Vegetable + Tofu Coconut
      Curry, *137,* 142, *143*
curry powder, Jamaican, 141
cutting boards, 10, 14

delicata squash, 84
dill
    Beef, Spinach + Feta
      Meatballs, *209,* 214, *215*
    Best Tuna Mac Salad, *189,*

198, *199*
    Braised Fish with Cream +
      Dill, *149, 154, 155*
    Chickpea + Spinach Rice, *165,*
      168, 169
    Springtime Chicken
      Meatballs, *209, 216, 217*
    Tahini Ranch Dressing, *23,*
      25, 27
dressings, salad
    basic formula, *22, 23*
    Creamy Lemon Dressing, *23,*
      24, 25
    Creamy Mustard Dressing,
      23, 25, 26
    Go-To Dressing, *29, 36, 37*
    Kimchi Dressing, *23, 25, 27*
    Pizzeria Vinaigrette, *23, 24,*
      25, 29
    Tahini Ranch Dressing, *23,*
      25, 27

Easiest Almond Cake, *263, 270,*
  271
eggplant
    Braised Eggplant with
      Tomatoes + Golden Raisins,
      149, 150, *151*
    Eggplant Parm Heroes, *233,*
      234, *235*
    Greek Orzo Bowl, *176–77,*
      180, *181*
eggs
    Bibimbap (Aka the Original
      Grain Bowl), *176–77,* 178,
      179
    Black Bean + Cheddar
      Cornbread Pie, *245, 252,*
      253
    Braised Spiced Lamb
      Meatballs, *209, 210, 211*
    Caesar Spaghetti, *189,* 190,
      191
    Chicken Francese, *221, 224,*
      225

eggs *(continued)*
    Easiest Almond Cake, *263,*
       270, 271
    Italian Wedding Soup, *113,*
       116, 117
    Morning Glory Muffins, *263,*
       264, 265
    Olive Oil + Buttermilk Loaf,
       263, 266–67, 269
    Pineapple Upside-Down Cake
       (A Cobbler, Inverted), *277,*
       286, 287, 288–89
    Raspberry + Chocolate
       Cobbler, *277, 284, 285*
    Roasted Chicken Pot Pie,
       245, 246, 247
    Turkey Meatballs with
       Gochujang Glaze, *209, 212,*
       213
escarole, 116
Espresso Wake-Up! Cake,
    Chocolate, *263, 272, 273*
Everything-Bagel Salmon +
    Smashed Potatoes, *233, 236,*
    237

Fajitas with Poblanos + Onions,
    Chicken, *221, 230, 231*
family bakery memories, 290–
    93
Farmers' Lunch Pasta, *189, 192,*
    193
farming experience, *106, 107–8,*
    109
Farro + Roasted Vegetable Salad,
    41, 48, 49
Fastest Chicken Noodle Soup,
    113, 114, 115
Favorite Broccoli Rabe, *71, 72, 73*
fennel, 44–45
    Shaved Fennel + Apple Salad,
       41, 46, 47
    Tomato, White Bean + Fennel
       Stew, *137, 146, 147*

fennel seeds
    Kinda Sicilian Spaghetti, *189,*
       200, *201*
    Tomato, White Bean + Fennel
       Stew, *137, 146, 147*
feta cheese
    Beef, Spinach + Feta
       Meatballs, *209, 214, 215*
    Chicken with Artichokes,
       Sun-Dried Tomatoes + Feta,
       221, 222, 223
    Chickpea + Spinach Rice, *165,*
       168, 169
    Feta + Rice-Stuffed Peppers,
       95, 96, 97
    Greek Orzo Bowl, *176–177,*
       180, *181*
    My Usual Chopped Salad, *29,*
       38, *39*
    Peppery Zucchini with
       Whipped Feta, *71, 78, 79*
    White Bean, Roasted Tomato
       + Polenta Pie, *245, 248,*
       249
    Winter Chopped Salad, *29,*
       36, 37
Fish + Cauliflower with Sicilian
    Tomato Salad, Roasted, *233,*
    238, 239
Fish Chowder, Frozen-, *113, 124,*
    125
Fish with Cream + Dill, Braised,
    149, 154, 155
five spice powder, Chinese, 226
flavorful ingredients, 19
freezing tips, 16
Fries, Sweet Potato, *233, 240,*
    241
fruity cobblers and crisps
    Apple + Cranberry Crisp, *277,*
       282, 283
    basic formula, 276, *277*
    Gingery Peach + Blueberry
       Cakey Cobbler, *277, 280,*
       281

    Pear, Cherry + Almond Crisp,
       277, 278, 279
    Pineapple Upside-Down Cake
       (A Cobbler, Inverted), *277,*
       286, 287, *288–89*
    Raspberry + Chocolate
       Cobbler, *277, 284, 285*
Full Fridge Club, 256–57,
    258–59

ginger, fresh
    Carrot Ginger Soup, *127, 129,*
       132
    Gingery Baby Bok Choy, *71,*
       80, 81
    Roasted Broccoli with Carrot-
       Miso Dressing, *83, 88, 89*
    Soy-Braised Tofu with
       Scallions, *149, 152, 153*
ginger, ground
    Carrot Ginger Soup, *127, 129,*
       132
    Gingery Peach + Blueberry
       Cakey Cobbler, *277, 280,*
       281
    Morning Glory Muffins, *263,*
       264, 265
goat cheese, 186
gochujang
    Bibimbap (Aka the Original
       Grain Bowl), *176–77, 178,*
       179
    Turkey Meatballs with
       Gochujang Glaze, *209, 212,*
       213
Go-To Dressing, *29, 36, 37*
grain bowls
    basic formula, 176, *176–77*
    Bibimbap (Aka the Original
       Grain Bowl), *176–77, 178,*
       179
    Child of the '90s Bowl, *176–*
       77, 186, 187
    Greek Orzo Bowl, *176–77,*
       180, *181*

Rice + Lentil Bowl with All the Toppings, *176–77*, *182*, 183

Shrimp + Grits Bowl, *176–77*, 184, *185*

Grandma's Raw Tomato Ziti, *189*, 196, *197*

Great Carrot Salad, A, *41*, 50, *51*

Great Tuna Sandwich, A, *54–55*, 56, 59, *60–61*

Greek Orzo Bowl, *176–77*, 180, *181*

green beans
 Child of the '90s Bowl, *176–77*, 186, *187*
 Roasted Green Beans with Walnuts + Lemon, *83*, 92, *93*

Grits Bowl, Shrimp +, *176–177*, 184, *185*

Gruyère cheese, 173

Haley's Savory Sprinkles, 118

Halloumi cheese, 183

ham, 62

Hoisin Chicken + Broccoli, Stir-Fried, *221*, 226, *227*

honey
 Carrots with Coriander + Cilantro, *71*, 76, *77*
 Creamy Lemon Dressing, *23*, 24, *25*
 Creamy Mustard Dressing, *23*, *25*, 26
 A Great Carrot Salad, *41*, 50, *51*
 Roasted Broccoli + Peanut Salad, *41*, 52, *53*
 Roasted Broccoli with Carrot-Miso Dressing, *83*, 88, *89*
 Roasted Brussels Sprouts with Sherry Vinaigrette + Manchego, *83*, *86*, *87*
 Roasted Squash Agrodolce, *83*, 84, *85*

Shaved Fennel + Apple Salad, *41*, 46, *47*

Soy-Braised Tofu with Scallions, 149, 152, *153*

Spicy Chicken with Lime + Cashews, *221*, 228, *229*

Sticky Pork with Broccoli, *233*, 242, *243*

Tahini Ranch Dressing, *23*, *25*, 27

Turkey Meatballs with Gochujang Glaze, *209*, 212, *213*

hummus, 59

iceberg lettuce
 BLT, *54–55*, 56, 57
 A Great Tuna Sandwich, *54–55*, 56, 59, *60–61*

immersion blenders, 17, 126

Italian Chopped Salad, *29*, 34, *35*

Italian Sausage + Ricotta Meatballs, *209*, 218, *219*

Italian Wedding Soup, 113, 116, *117*

Jennie's Curried Chicken + Potatoes, *137*, *140*, 141

kale
 Farmers' Lunch Pasta, *189*, 192, *193*
 Vegan Kale Caesar with Crispy Chickpeas, *29*, 32, *33*
 Winter Chopped Salad, *29*, 36, *37*

ketchup
 Cold Roast Chicken Sandwich, *54–55*, 58, 59, *60–61*
 Sticky Pork with Broccoli, *233*, 242, *243*

kimchi
 Bibimbap (Aka the Original Grain Bowl), *176–77*, 178, *179*

Chicken + Kimchi Rice, 165, 170, *171*

Cucumber + Avocado Salad, *41*, 42, *43*

Kimchi Dressing, *23*, *25*, 27

kitchen tools, 160–61, *298*

Lamb Meatballs, Braised Spiced, *209*, 210, *211*

Lemon, Roasted Green Beans with Walnuts +, *83*, 92, *93*

Lemon Dressing, Creamy, *23*, 24, *25*

lentils
 Lentil + Sweet Potato Shepherd's Pie, *245*, 250, *251*
 Rice + Lentil Bowl with All the Toppings, *176–77*, *182*, 183

lettuce-based salads
 basic formula, 28, *29*
 Classic Caesar with Big Crunchy Croutons, *29*, 30, *31*
 Italian Chopped Salad, *29*, 34, *35*
 My Usual Chopped Salad, *29*, 38, *39*
 Vegan Kale Caesar with Crispy Chickpeas, *29*, 32, *33*
 Winter Chopped Salad, *29*, 36, *37*

lima beans, 74

limes/lime juice
 Chicken Fajitas with Poblanos + Onions, *221*, 230, 231
 Creamy Tomato + Coconut Soup, *127*, 128, *133*, 134, 134
 Spicy Chicken with Lime + Cashews, *221*, 228, *229*

Long Season Farm, *106*, 107–8, *109*, 194–95

main dishes
 meatballs, 208–19

main dishes *(continued)*
  sautéed chicken dishes, 220–31
  savory pies, 244–55
  sheet pan dinners, 232–43
Manchego, Roasted Brussels Sprouts with Sherry Vinaigrette +, *83, 86, 87*
maple syrup, 272
marinara sauce, 218
measuring tips, 26
meatballs
  basic formula, 208, *209*
  Beef, Spinach + Feta Meatballs, *209,* 214, *215*
  Braised Spiced Lamb Meatballs, *209,* 210, *211*
  Italian Sausage + Ricotta Meatballs, *209,* 218, *219*
  Springtime Chicken Meatballs, *209,* 216, *217*
  Turkey Meatballs with Gochujang Glaze, *209,* 212, *213*
menu planning suggestions, 294, *294–95, 296–97*
Microplane zesters, 17
Minestrone-ish, *113,* 118, *119*
mint, 216
miso paste, 88
Morning Glory Muffins, *263, 264,* 265
mozzarella cheese
  Eggplant Parm Heroes, *233, 234, 235*
  Grandma's Raw Tomato Ziti, *189,* 196, *197*
Muffins, Morning Glory, *263, 264,* 265
mushrooms
  Mushroom Cacciatore, *137,* 138, *139*
  Mushrooms Rockefeller, *95,* 100, *101*
  Mushroom Swiss Burger Rice, *165, 172, 173*

mustard
  Creamy Mustard Dressing, *23, 25,* 26
  Everything-Bagel Salmon + Smashed Potatoes, *233, 236,* 237
  A Great Tuna Sandwich, *54–55,* 56, 59, *60–61*
My Favorite Veggie Sandwich, *54–55,* 58, 59, *60–61*
My Usual Chopped Salad, *29, 38, 39*

non-lettuce salads
  basic formula, 40, *41*
  Cucumber + Avocado Salad, *41, 42, 43*
  Farro + Roasted Vegetable Salad, *41, 48, 49*
  A Great Carrot Salad, *41,* 50, *51*
  Roasted Broccoli + Peanut Salad, *41,* 52, *53*
  Shaved Fennel + Apple Salad, *41, 46, 47*
nuts. *See also specific nuts*
  Farro + Roasted Vegetable Salad, *41, 48, 49*
  Shaved Fennel + Apple Salad, *41, 46, 47*

oats, rolled
  Apple + Cranberry Crisp, *277, 282,* 283
  Pear, Cherry + Almond Crisp, *277, 278, 279*
offset spatulas, 18
Old Bay Seasoning
  Frozen-Fish Chowder, *113, 124,* 125
  Shrimp + Bacon Rice, *165, 174, 175*
olive oil, bulk, 16
Olive Oil + Buttermilk Loaf, *263, 266–67,* 269

olives
  Best Tuna Mac Salad, *189, 198, 199*
  Braised Pork with Apricots + Green Olives, *149, 158, 159*
  A Great Carrot Salad, *41,* 50, *51*
  Greek Orzo Bowl, *176–77,* 180, *181*
  Italian Chopped Salad, *29,* 34, *35*
  Mushroom Cacciatore, *137, 138, 139*
  Roasted Fish + Cauliflower with Sicilian Tomato Salad, *233, 238, 239*
  White Bean, Roasted Tomato + Polenta Pie, *245,* 248, *249*
one-bowl batters
  basic formula, 262, *263*
  Chocolate Espresso Wake-Up! Cake, *263,* 272, *273*
  Easiest Almond Cake, *263,* 270, *271*
  Morning Glory Muffins, *263, 264,* 265
  Olive Oil + Buttermilk Loaf, *263, 266–67, 268,* 269
  Pumpkin Chocolate Chip Bread, *263,* 274, *275*
one-pot rice dishes
  basic formula, 164, *165*
  Chicken + Kimchi Rice, *165, 170, 171*
  Chickpea + Spinach Rice, *165, 168,* 169
  Chorizo + Sofrito Rice, *165, 166, 167*
  Mushroom Swiss Burger Rice, *165, 172,* 173
  Shrimp + Bacon Rice, *165, 174, 175*
Onions, Chicken Fajitas with Poblanos +, *221, 230, 231*

onions, red
  Best Tuna Mac Salad, *189*,
    198, *199*
  Lentil + Sweet Potato
    Shepherd's Pie, *245*, *250*,
    251
  Winter Chopped Salad, *29*,
    36, 37
online cooking classes, 64, *65*,
  66–67, *67*
oregano
  Beef, Spinach + Feta
    Meatballs, *209*, 214, *215*
  Chicken Scarpariello, *149*,
    156, 157
  Chicken with Artichokes,
    Sun-Dried Tomatoes + Feta,
    221, 222, *223*
  Chickpea + Spinach Rice, *165*,
    168, 169
  Feta + Rice-Stuffed Peppers,
    95, *96*, 97
  Italian Wedding Soup, *113*,
    116, *117*
  Minestrone-ish, *113*, 118, *119*
  Mushroom Cacciatore, *137*,
    138, 139
  Pizzeria Vinaigrette, *23*, 24,
    25
  White Bean, Roasted Tomato
    + Polenta Pie, *245*, 248,
    249

panko breadcrumbs
  Braised Spiced Lamb
    Meatballs, *209*, 210, *211*
  Haley's Savory Sprinkles, 118
  Italian Wedding Soup, *113*,
    116, *117*
  Kinda Sicilian Spaghetti, *189*,
    200, *201*
  Mushrooms Rockefeller, *95*,
    100, *101*
  Tomatoes Casino, *95*, 102,
    103

Turkey Meatballs with
  Gochujang Glaze, *209*, 212,
  213
paprika
  Braised Spiced Lamb
    Meatballs, *209*, 210, *211*
  Chicken with Artichokes,
    Sun-Dried Tomatoes + Feta,
    221, 222, *223*
  Fastest Chicken Noodle
    Soup, *113*, *114*, 115
  Rice + Lentil Bowl with All the
    Toppings, *176–177*, *182*, 183
  Vegan Kale Caesar with
    Crispy Chickpeas, *29*, 32, *33*
Parmesan cheese
  Caesar Spaghetti, *189*, 190,
    191
  Classic Caesar with Big
    Crunchy Croutons, *29*, 30,
    31
  Eggplant Parm Heroes, *233*,
    234, *235*
  Haley's Savory Sprinkles, 118
  Italian Sausage + Ricotta
    Meatballs, *209*, 218, *219*
  Kinda Sicilian Spaghetti, *189*,
    200, *201*
  Minestrone-ish, *113*, 118, *119*
  Mushrooms Rockefeller, *95*,
    100, *101*
  Shaved Fennel + Apple Salad,
    41, 46, *47*
  White Bean, Roasted Tomato
    + Polenta Pie, *245*, 248,
    249
parsley
  Best Tuna Mac Salad, *189*,
    198, *199*
  Caesar Spaghetti, *189*, 190,
    191
  Chicken Francese, *221*, 224,
    225
  Farmers' Lunch Pasta, *189*,
    192, *193*

A Great Carrot Salad, *41*,
  50, *51*
Italian Sausage + Ricotta
  Meatballs, *209*, 218, *219*
Kinda Sicilian Spaghetti, *189*,
  200, *201*
Roasted Fish + Cauliflower
  with Sicilian Tomato Salad,
  233, *238*, 239
Tomatoes Casino, *95*, 102,
  103
pasta
  Fastest Chicken Noodle
    Soup, *113*, *114*, 115
  Greek Orzo Bowl, *176–77*,
    180, *181*
  Italian Wedding Soup, *113*,
    116, *117*
  Minestrone-ish, *113*, 118, *119*
  quick pastas, 188–201
Peach + Blueberry Cakey
  Cobbler, Gingery, *277*, 280,
  281
peanuts/peanut butter
  Roasted Broccoli + Peanut
    Salad, *41*, 52, *53*
  Roasted Sweet Potatoes with
    Salsa Macha, *83*, 90, *91*
Pear, Cherry + Almond Crisp,
  277, 278, *279*
pecans
  Child of the '90s Bowl, *176–*
    77, 186, *187*
  Morning Glory Muffins, *263*,
    264, 265
pecorino cheese
  Italian Sausage + Ricotta
    Meatballs, *209*, 218, *219*
  Italian Wedding Soup, *113*,
    116, *117*
  Twice-Baked Cacio e Pepe
    Potatoes, *95*, 98, 99
pepperoncini peppers
  A Great Tuna Sandwich,
    54–55, 56, 59, *60–61*

pepperoncini peppers (continued)
Italian Chopped Salad, 29, 34, 35
peppers, cherry
Chicken Scarpariello, 149, 156, 157
Cold Roast Chicken Sandwich, 54–55, 58, 59, 60–61
peppers, red, 34
Peppery Zucchini with Whipped Feta, 71, 78, 79
pesto
Child of the '90s Bowl, 176–77, 186, 187
Minestrone-ish, 113, 118, 119
pies. See savory pies
pimentón
BBQ Tofu + Sweet Potato Fries, 233, 240, 241
Black Bean + Cheddar Cornbread Pie, 245, 252, 253
Chicken Fajitas with Poblanos + Onions, 221, 230, 231
Chorizo + Sofrito Rice, 165, 166, 167
Lentil + Sweet Potato Shepherd's Pie, 245, 250, 251
Spiced Chickpea Squash Bowls, 95, 104, 105
Turkey + Green Chile Chili, 137, 144, 145
pineapple
Morning Glory Muffins, 263, 264, 265
Pineapple Upside-Down Cake (A Cobbler, Inverted), 277, 286, 287, 288–89
pine nuts, 200
Pizzeria Vinaigrette, 23, 24, 25, 29
Poblanos + Onions, Chicken Fajitas with, 221, 230, 231

polenta, 248
pomegranate seeds, 183
porcini powder, 138
pork shoulder, 158
pork tenderloin, 242
potatoes
Everything-Bagel Salmon + Smashed Potatoes, 233, 236, 237
Frozen-Fish Chowder, 113, 124, 125
Jennie's Curried Chicken + Potatoes, 137, 140, 141
Red Curry Corn Soup, 127, 128, 133, 133
Twice-Baked Cacio e Pepe Potatoes, 95, 98, 99
Pot Pie, Roasted Chicken, 245, 246, 247
preheating tips, 18
pressure cookers, 160–61
provolone cheese, 34
puff pastry, 160
pumpkin pie spice, 274
pumpkin purée, 274
pumpkin seeds, 37, 130
pureed soups
basic formula, 126, 127
Carrot Ginger Soup, 127, 129, 132
Creamy Tomato + Coconut Soup, 127, 128, 133, 134, 134
Red Curry Corn Soup, 127, 128, 133, 133
Roasted Squash Soup, 127, 129, 130, 131
Spicy Sweet Potato Soup, 127, 128–29, 133, 135

queer cooking, 256–57, 257, 258–59
quick pastas
basic formula, 188, 189
Best Tuna Mac Salad, 189, 198, 199

Caesar Spaghetti, 189, 190, 191
Farmers' Lunch Pasta, 189, 192, 193
Grandma's Raw Tomato Ziti, 189, 196, 197
Kinda Sicilian Spaghetti, 189, 200, 201

raisins
Braised Eggplant with Tomatoes + Golden Raisins, 149, 150, 151
A Great Carrot Salad, 41, 50, 51
Kinda Sicilian Spaghetti, 189, 200, 201
Morning Glory Muffins, 263, 264, 265
My Usual Chopped Salad, 29, 38, 39
Raspberry + Chocolate Cobbler, 277, 284, 285
Red Curry Corn Soup, 127, 128, 133, 133
red pepper flakes
Chicken + Kimchi Rice, 165, 170, 171
Cucumber + Avocado Salad, 41, 42, 43
Favorite Broccoli Rabe, 71, 72, 73
Kimchi Dressing, 23, 25, 27
Kinda Sicilian Spaghetti, 189, 200, 201
red pepper paste, Korean. See gochujang
red wine, 138
rice
Bibimbap (Aka the Original Grain Bowl), 176–77, 178, 179
Chicken + Kimchi Rice, 165, 170, 171

Chickpea + Spinach Rice, *165,* *168,* 169

Child of the '90s Bowl, *176–77,* 186, *187*

Chorizo + Sofrito Rice, *165,* 166, *167*

Feta + Rice-Stuffed Peppers, *95,* 96, *97*

Mushroom Swiss Burger Rice, *165,* *172,* 173

one-pot rice dishes, 164–75

Rice + Lentil Bowl with All the Toppings, *176–77,* *182,* 183

Shrimp + Bacon Rice, *165,* *174,* 175

ricotta cheese

Farmers' Lunch Pasta, *189,* 192, *193*

Italian Sausage + Ricotta Meatballs, *209,* 218, *219*

Kinda Sicilian Spaghetti, *189,* 200, *201*

Roasted Chicken Pot Pie, *245,* *246,* 247

Roasted Fish + Cauliflower with Sicilian Tomato Salad, *233, 238,* 239

roasted vegetables

basic formula, 82, *83*

Farro + Roasted Vegetable Salad, *41,* 48, *49*

Roasted Broccoli + Peanut Salad, *41,* 52, *53*

Roasted Broccoli with Carrot-Miso Dressing, *83,* 88, *89*

Roasted Brussels Sprouts with Sherry Vinaigrette + Manchego, *83, 86,* 87

Roasted Green Beans with Walnuts + Lemon, *83,* 92, *93*

Roasted Squash Agrodolce, *83,* 84, *85*

Roasted Squash Soup, *127,* *129,* 130, *131*

Roasted Sweet Potatoes with Salsa Macha, *83, 90, 91*

romaine lettuce

Best Ham Sandwich, *54–55,* 62, *63*

Classic Caesar with Big Crunchy Croutons, *29,* 30, *31*

Italian Chopped Salad, *29,* 34, *35*

My Usual Chopped Salad, *29,* 38, *39*

rosemary, 138, 158

salads, 22–53

Best Tuna Mac Salad, *189,* 198, *199*

lettuce-based salads, 28–39

non-lettuce salads, 40–53

Roasted Fish + Cauliflower with Sicilian Tomato Salad, *233, 238,* 239

salad dressings, 22–27, *29,* 36, *37*

salami, 34

Salmon + Smashed Potatoes, Everything-Bagel, *233, 236,* 237

Salsa Macha, Roasted Sweet Potatoes with, *83, 90, 91*

sambal/chile paste, 228, 242

sandwiches, 54–63

basic formula, 54, *54–55*

Best Ham Sandwich, *54–55,* 62, *63*

BLT, *54–55,* 56, *57*

Cold Roast Chicken Sandwich, *54–55,* 58, *59,* *60–61*

Eggplant Parm Heroes, *233,* *234, 235*

A Great Tuna Sandwich, *54–55,* 56, 59, *60–61*

My Favorite Veggie Sandwich, *54–55,* 58, 59, *60–61*

sausage

Biscuits + Gravy Pie, *245, 254, 255*

Chicken Scarpariello, *149, 156, 157*

Italian Sausage + Ricotta Meatballs, *209, 218, 219*

sautéed chicken dishes

basic formula, 220, *221*

Chicken Fajitas with Poblanos + Onions, *221, 230, 231*

Chicken Francese, *221, 224, 225*

Chicken with Artichokes, Sun-Dried Tomatoes + Feta, *221, 222, 223*

Spicy Chicken with Lime + Cashews, *221, 228, 229*

Stir-Fried Hoisin Chicken + Broccoli, *221, 226, 227*

savory pies

basic formula, 244, *245*

Biscuits + Gravy Pie, *245, 254, 255*

Black Bean + Cheddar Cornbread Pie, *245, 252, 253*

Lentil + Sweet Potato Shepherd's Pie, *245, 250,* 251

Roasted Chicken Pot Pie, *245, 246, 247*

White Bean, Roasted Tomato + Polenta Pie, *245, 248, 249*

scallions

Bibimbap (Aka the Original Grain Bowl), *176–77,* 178, *179*

Gingery Baby Bok Choy, *71, 80, 81*

Roasted Broccoli + Peanut Salad, *41,* 52, *53*

Shrimp + Grits Bowl, *176–77,* 184, *185*

scallions (continued)
Soy-Braised Tofu with Scallions, 149, 152, 153

sesame seeds
Bibimbap (Aka the Original Grain Bowl), 176–77, 178, 179
Gingery Baby Bok Choy, 71, 80, 81
Roasted Sweet Potatoes with Salsa Macha, 83, 90, 91

Shaved Fennel + Apple Salad, 41, 46, 47

sheet pan dinners
basic formula, 232, 233
BBQ Tofu + Sweet Potato Fries, 233, 240, 241
Eggplant Parm Heroes, 233, 234, 235
Everything-Bagel Salmon + Smashed Potatoes, 233, 236, 237
Roasted Fish + Cauliflower with Sicilian Tomato Salad, 233, 238, 239
Sticky Pork with Broccoli, 233, 242, 243

Shepherd's Pie, Lentil + Sweet Potato, 245, 250, 251

Shrimp + Bacon Rice, 165, 174, 175

Shrimp + Grits Bowl, 176–77, 184, 185

Skillet Succotash, 71, 74, 75

soups
brothy soups, 112–21, 124–25
pureed soups, 126–35

sour cream
Pineapple Upside-Down Cake (A Cobbler, Inverted), 277, 286, 287, 288–89
Roasted Squash Soup, 127, 129, 130, 131
Spicy Sweet Potato Soup, 127, 128–29, 133, 135

Twice-Baked Cacio e Pepe Potatoes, 95, 98, 99

Soy-Braised Tofu with Scallions, 149, 152, 153

Spiced Chickpea Squash Bowls, 95, 104, 105

Spicy Chicken with Lime + Cashews, 221, 228, 229

Spicy Sweet Potato Soup, 127, 128–29, 133, 135

spinach
Beef, Spinach + Feta Meatballs, 209, 214, 215
Chickpea + Spinach Rice, 165, 168, 169
Feta + Rice-Stuffed Peppers, 95, 96, 97
Italian Wedding Soup, 113, 116, 117
Mushrooms Rockefeller, 95, 100, 101

spinach, baby, 178

Springtime Chicken Meatballs, 209, 216, 217

squash. See also specific squash; zucchini
Rice + Lentil Bowl with All the Toppings, 176–177, 182, 183

stews
basic formula, 136, 137
Jennie's Curried Chicken + Potatoes, 137, 140, 141
Mushroom Cacciatore, 137, 138, 139
Tomato, White Bean + Fennel Stew, 137, 146, 147
Turkey + Green Chile Chili, 137, 144, 145
Vegetable + Tofu Coconut Curry, 137, 142, 143

sticky ingredients/jars, 15

Sticky Pork with Broccoli, 233, 242, 243

Stir-Fried Hoisin Chicken + Broccoli, 221, 226, 227

stovetop vegetables
basic formula, 70, 71
Carrots with Coriander + Cilantro, 71, 76, 77
Favorite Broccoli Rabe, 71, 72, 73
Gingery Baby Bok Choy, 71, 80, 81
Peppery Zucchini with Whipped Feta, 71, 78, 79
Skillet Succotash, 71, 74, 75

stuffed vegetables
basic formula, 94, 95
Feta + Rice-Stuffed Peppers, 95, 96, 97
Mushrooms Rockefeller, 95, 100, 101
Spiced Chickpea Squash Bowls, 95, 104, 105
Tomatoes Casino, 95, 102, 103
Twice-Baked Cacio e Pepe Potatoes, 95, 98, 99

Succotash, Skillet, 71, 74, 75

sweet potatoes
BBQ Tofu + Sweet Potato Fries, 233, 240, 241
Lentil + Sweet Potato Shepherd's Pie, 245, 250, 251
Roasted Sweet Potatoes with Salsa Macha, 83, 90, 91
Spicy Sweet Potato Soup, 127, 128–29, 133, 135

tahini
Rice + Lentil Bowl with All the Toppings, 176–77, 182, 183
Springtime Chicken Meatballs, 209, 216, 217
Tahini Ranch Dressing, 23, 25, 27
Winter Chopped Salad, 29, 36, 37

teaching experiences, 64, 65, 66–67, 67
tofu
  BBQ Tofu + Sweet Potato Fries, 233, 240, 241
  Soy-Braised Tofu with Scallions, 149, 152, 153
  Vegetable + Tofu Coconut Curry, 137, 142, 143
tomatoes
  Black Bean + Cheddar Cornbread Pie, 245, 252, 253
  BLT, 54–55, 56, 57
  Braised Eggplant with Tomatoes + Golden Raisins, 149, 150, 151
  Braised Spiced Lamb Meatballs, 209, 210, 211
  Creamy Tomato + Coconut Soup, 127, 128, 133, 134, 134
  Lentil + Sweet Potato Shepherd's Pie, 245, 250, 251
  Minestrone-ish, 113, 118, 119
  Mushroom Cacciatore, 137, 138, 139
  Spiced Chickpea Squash Bowls, 95, 104, 105
  Tomato, White Bean + Fennel Stew, 137, 146, 147
  Tomatoes Casino, 95, 102, 103
  Turkey + Green Chile Chili, 137, 144, 145
tomatoes, cherry
  Child of the '90s Bowl, 176–77, 186, 187
  cutting tips, 196
  Grandma's Raw Tomato Ziti, 189, 196, 197
  Roasted Fish + Cauliflower with Sicilian Tomato Salad, 233, 238, 239
  Skillet Succotash, 71, 74, 75

White Bean, Roasted Tomato + Polenta Pie, 245, 248, 249
tomatoes, sun-dried, 222
tomato paste
  Black Bean + Cheddar Cornbread Pie, 245, 252, 253
  Braised Spiced Lamb Meatballs, 209, 210, 211
  Chorizo + Sofrito Rice, 165, 166, 167
  Minestrone-ish, 113, 118, 119
  Mushroom Cacciatore, 137, 138, 139
tomato sauce, 234
tuna
  Best Tuna Mac Salad, 189, 198, 199
  A Great Tuna Sandwich, 54–55, 56, 59, 60–61
turkey, ground
  Italian Sausage + Ricotta Meatballs, 209, 218, 219
  Turkey + Green Chile Chili, 137, 144, 145
  Turkey Meatballs with Gochujang Glaze, 209, 212, 213
Twice-Baked Cacio e Pepe Potatoes, 95, 98, 99

Upside-Down Cake (A Cobbler, Inverted), Pineapple, 277, 286, 287, 288–289

Vegan Kale Caesar with Crispy Chickpeas, 29, 32, 33
vegetables. See also specific vegetables
  My Favorite Veggie Sandwich, 54–55, 58, 59, 60–61
  Roasted Broccoli + Peanut Salad, 41, 52, 53
  roasted vegetables, 82–93

stovetop vegetables, 70–81
stuffed vegetables, 94–105
Vegetable + Tofu Coconut Curry, 137, 142, 143
vegetables, mixed
  Farro + Roasted Vegetable Salad, 41, 48, 49
  Roasted Chicken Pot Pie, 245, 246, 247
  Vegetable + Tofu Coconut Curry, 137, 142, 143
vinaigrettes
  Pizzeria, 23, 24, 25, 29
  sherry, 83, 86, 97

Walnuts + Lemon, Roasted Green Beans with, 83, 92, 93
White Bean, Roasted Tomato + Polenta Pie, 245, 248, 249
White Bean + Fennel Stew, Tomato, 137, 146, 147
white wine
  Braised Fish with Cream + Dill, 149, 154, 155
  Chicken Francese, 221, 224, 225
  Chicken Scarpariello, 149, 156, 157
  Skillet Succotash, 71, 74, 75
Winter Chopped Salad, 29, 36, 37

yeast, nutritional, 32
yogurt
  Beef, Spinach + Feta Meatballs, 209, 214, 215
  Creamy Lemon Dressing, 23, 24, 25

zucchini
  Peppery Zucchini with Whipped Feta, 71, 78, 79
  Skillet Succotash, 71, 74, 75
  Springtime Chicken Meatballs, 209, 216, 217

BEHIND THE SCENES!

HERE'S THE NAPKIN I WROTE INITIAL NOTES FOR THE BOOK ON!

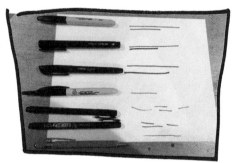

CHOOSING THE RIGHT MARKER FOR THE CHARTS!

AN EARLY COVER MOCK-UP FROM MY MOM!

MY PARENTS GETTING ALL THE PAGES UP ON A WALL!

A PHOTO GRACE TOOK OF ME
TAKING A PHOTO OF SOUP! I TOOK
NEARLY ALL THE PHOTOS IN THE BOOK!

YOU'VE

GOT THIS!

XOXO, Julia

ABOUT THE AUTHOR

Julia Turshen is a *New York Times* bestselling cookbook author. Her last book, *Simply Julia*, is an International Association of Culinary Professionals (IACP) award-winning national bestseller. Julia has written for multiple publications, including the *New York Times*, the *Washington Post*, and *Vogue*. She is the founder of Equity at the Table (EATT), an inclusive digital directory of women/nonbinary individuals in food, and the host and producer of the IACP-nominated podcast *Keep Calm and Cook On*, which the *New York Times* has called "an antidote to diet culture." *Epicurious* has named Julia one of the "100 Greatest Home Cooks of All Time." She sits on the Kitchen Cabinet Advisory Board for the Smithsonian's National Museum of American History and is a member of God's Love We Deliver's Culinary Council. She writes a weekly newsletter, teaches live cooking classes nearly every Sunday afternoon, and is a competitive powerlifter. Julia lives in the Hudson Valley with her spouse, Grace, and their many pets.

JULIA TURSHEN is the bestselling author of *Simply Julia*, *Now & Again*, *Feed the Resistance*, and *Small Victories* and has coauthored numerous other cookbooks, including the James Beard Award–winning *In Bibi's Kitchen*. She hosts the International Association of Culinary Professionals–nominated podcast *Keep Calm and Cook On* and has written for the *New York Times*, the *Washington Post*, the *Wall Street Journal*, *Vogue*, *Bon Appétit*, *Food & Wine*, *Saveur*, and more. She lives in the Hudson Valley with her spouse, Grace, and their many pets.